RELIABILITY AND VALIDITY IN QUALITATIVE RESEARCH

JEROME KIRK
University of California, Irvine

MARC L. MILLER
University of Washington

Qualitative Research Methods,
Volume 1

SAGE PUBLICATIONS
The International Professional Publishers
Newbury Park   London   New Delhi

For information address:

SAGE Publications, Inc.
2455 Teller Road
Newbury Park, California 91320

SAGE Publications Ltd.
6 Bonhill Street
London EC2A 4PU
United Kingdom

SAGE Publications India Pvt. Ltd.
M-32 Market
Greater Kailash I
New Delhi 110 048 India

International Standard Book Number 0-8039-2560-3
0-8039-2470-4 (pbk.)

Library of Congress Catalog Card No. 85-2412

93 94 15 14 13 12 11

When citing a University Paper, please use the proper form. Remember to cite the correct
Sage University Paper series title and include the paper number. One of the following
formats can be adapted (depending on the style manual used):

(1) AGAR, MICHAEL H. (1985) Speaking of Ethnography. Sage University Paper
series on Qualitative Research Methods, Volume 2. Beverly Hills, CA: Sage.

or

(2) Agar, Michael H. 1985. *Speaking of ethnography.* Sage University Paper series on
Qualitative Research Methods (Vol. 2). Beverly Hills, CA: Sage.

CONTENTS

SERIES INTRODUCTION

Contrast and irony provide the definitional context for this series of monographs on qualitative methods. Contrast is inevitable because the label itself makes sense only when set against something it is not. Irony is also inevitable because the denotative contrast between the qualitative and quantitative is so often misleading, if not downright false. The mandate for the series is then paradoxical. We wish to highlight the distinctions between methods thought to be qualitative and quantitative, but also to demonstrate that such distinctions typically break down when subject to scrutiny. Alongside the Sage Series on Quantitative Applications in the Social Sciences comes the Sage Series on Qualitative Research Methods, but the wise reader had best intermingle the monographs of the two sets rather than stack them on separate shelves.

One way of approaching the paradox is to think of qualitative methods as procedures for counting to one. Deciding what is to count as a unit of analysis is fundamentally an interpretive issue requiring judgment and choice. It is, however, a choice that cuts to the core of qualitative methods—where meanings rather than frequencies assume paramount significance. Qualitative work is blatantly interpretive; but, as the work in this series demonstrates, there are a number of increasingly sophisticated procedures to guide the interpretive acts of social researchers.

The monographs in this series go beyond the short confessionals usually found in the methodology sections of research reports. They also go beyond the rather flat, programmatic treatments afforded qualitative methods in most research textbooks. Not only are qualitative methods becoming more variegated, going well beyond the traditional look, listen, and learn

6

dicta issued by traditional field researchers, they are also being shaped more distinctly by explicit philosophical and moral positions. This series seeks to elaborate both qualitative techniques and the intellectual grounds on which they stand.

The series is designed for the novice eager to learn about specific modes of social inquiry as well as for the veteran researcher curious about the widening range of social science methods. Each contribution extends the boundaries of methodological discourse, but not at the expense of losing the uninitiated. The aim is to minimize jargon, make analytic premises visible, provide concrete examples, and limit the scope of each volume with precision and restraint. These are, to be sure, introductory monographs, but each allows for the development of a lively research theme with subtlety, detail, and illustration. To a large extent, each monograph deals with the specific ways qualitative researchers establish norms and justify their craft. We think the time is right to display the rather remarkable growth of qualitative methods in both number and reflective consideration. We are confident that readers of this series will agree.

—*John Van Maanen*
Peter K. Manning
Marc L. Miller

EDITORS' INTRODUCTION

The most venerable tradition among qualitative methods is unquestionably participant observation. Strictly speaking, this stiff but precise phrase refers more to the oscillating situation of researchers as they move in, through, and out of the field than it does to a particular research technique. Jerome Kirk and Marc Miller, in this first volume of the Sage Series on Qualitative Research Methods, classify fieldwork situations in terms of a highly general process model of participant-observation research. They do so well within the conventional wisdom of what constitutes science and, as their title suggests, concern themselves largely with issues surrounding the scientific status of field data. A sort of flowchart of social research, from discovery to analysis, emerges in this monograph along with a guide to the critical issues and themes that characteristically mark each designated phase of the process. A nondoctrinaire but distinctly pragmatic research philosophy accompanies their efforts to bring rhyme and reason to the often chaotic circumstances surrounding participant observation.

RELIABILITY AND VALIDITY IN QUALITATIVE RESEARCH

JEROME KIRK
University of California, Irvine
MARC L. MILLER
University of Washington

1. OBJECTIVITY IN QUALITATIVE RESEARCH

Qualitative research is a particular tradition in social science that fundamentally depends on watching people in their own territory and interacting with them in their own language, on their own terms. As identified with sociology, cultural anthropology, and political science, among other disciplines, qualitative research has been seen to be "naturalistic," "ethnographic," and "participatory."

It should be remarked at the outset that the term "qualitative" in reference to this tradition has led to a variety of misunderstandings. Technically, a "qualitative observation" identifies the presence or absence of something, in contrast to "quantitative observation," which involves measuring the degree to which some feature is present. To identify something, the observer must know what qualifies as that thing, or that kind of thing. This entails counting to one. It follows from this narrow consideration that qualitative research would denote any research based on percentages, means, chi-squares, and other statistics appropriate to cardinal, or counting, numbers.

On the other hand, "quality" connotes the nature, as opposed to the "quantity," or amount, of a thing. According to this equally limited consideration, qualitative research would denote any research distinguished by the absence of counting.

AUTHORS' NOTE: We relish this opportunity to apologize to all those we fear to acknowledge.

9

10

These two plausible definitions directly contradict one another. Neither suits the present purpose very well. Whether or not a number gets used in the process of recording and analyzing observations is an entirely abstract issue. By our pragmatic view, qualitative research does imply a commitment to field activities. It does not imply a commitment to innumeracy. Qualitative research is an empirical, socially located phenomenon, defined by its own history, not simply a residual grab-bag comprising all things that are "not quantitative." Its diverse expressions include analytic induction, content analysis, semiotics, hermeneutics, elite interviewing, the study of life histories, and certain archival, computer, and statistical manipulations. One purpose of the series of which this volume is a part is to elaborate on these and other possibilities.

The accumulated wisdom of the academic tradition of qualitative research is largely a formal distillation of sophisticated techniques employed by all sorts of professionals—adventurers, detectives, journalists, spies—to find out things about people. Necessarily, the formal tradition has been accompanied by certain distinctive orientations. Qualitative research is socially concerned, cosmopolitan, and, above all, objective.

Objectivity

"Objectivity," too, is an ambiguous concept. In one sense, it refers to the heuristic assumption, common in the natural sciences, that everything in the universe can, in principle, be explained in terms of causality. In the social sciences, this assumption often seems to miss the point, for much of what social scientists try to explain is the consequence of inner existential choices made by people. In ordinary language, when we ask "why" a person acts as he or she does, we are generally inquiring teleologically about his or her purposes. Indeed, if knowledge itself is taken to be merely the inevitable consequence of some mechanistic chain of cause and effect, its logical status would seem to be compromised.

In another sense, "objectivity" refers to taking an intellectual risk—the risk of being demonstrably wrong. Popper's model of the *hypothetico-deductive method* exemplifies this connotation. According to Popper (1959: 42), the scientist prepares to test theories by deriving from them hypotheses that can in principle break down when applied in the real world:

> What characterizes the empirical method is its manner of exposing to falsification, in every conceivable way, the system to be tested. Its aim is not to save the lives of untenable systems but, on the contrary, to select the one which is by comparison the fittest, by exposing them all to the fiercest struggle for survival.

Even in Popper's sophisticated formulation, the hypothetico-deductive model is rather an inaccurate and schoolmarmish description of what scientists do, but it properly contrasts the scientific enterprise with others (such as art or ethics) in which practitioners do not routinely subject their theories to that sort of empirical risk, or their egos to the potential of battery not only by the arguments of intellectual adversaries but also by the de-monstrative refutation of the empirical world.

It is in this latter sense that qualitative researchers have always celebrated objectivity. A commitment to objectivity does not imply a desire to "objectify" the subject matter by "over-measurement" (Etzioni, 1964), or to facilitate authoritarian social relationships by treating human beings as though they *were* certain features they may happen to have.[1] It does not presuppose any radically positivist view of the world; it emphatically eschews the search for final, absolute "truth," preferring to leave such an enterprise to philosophers and theologians.

The assumptions underlying the search for objectivity are simple. There is a world of empirical reality out there. The way we perceive and understand that world is largely up to us, but the world does not tolerate all understandings of it equally (so that the individual who believes he or she can halt a speeding train with his or her bare hands may be punished by the world for acting on that understanding). There is a long-standing intel-lectual community for which it seems worthwhile to try to figure out collectively how best to talk about the empirical world, by means of incremental, partial improvements in understanding.

Often, these improvements come about by identifying ambiguity in prior, apparently clear, views, or by showing that there are cases in which some alternative view works better. Previously held views are not in general taken to be refuted by such contributions, but complemented by them. "Truth" (or what provisionally passes for truth at a particular time) is thus bounded both by the tolerance of empirical reality and by the consensus of the scholarly community (Blumer, 1968).

Natural science is strongly identified with a commitment to objectivity. Like natural science, qualitative social research is pluralistic. A variety of models may be applied to the same object for different purposes. A man may be an object of a certain mass and size to an engineer, a bundle of neuroses to the psychologist, a walking pharmacy to the biochemist, and a bank account with desires to an economist. Light may have a frequency or (in this case, by a describable transformation) consist of photons. Water is the canonical acid and the ultimate primitive base. Natural human vision is binocular, for seeing the same thing simultaneously from more than one perspective gives a fuller understanding of its depth. The reason Einstein originally called his theory of relativity the Theory of Invariance is because though everything displays different aspects to different viewpoints, some features remain the same.

Plan of This Book

The several points in this orientation are easily reviewed. Qualitative research is a sociological and anthropological tradition of inquiry. Most critically, qualitative research involves sustained interaction with the people being studied in their own language, and on their own turf. Less important is whether or not, or at what level of sophistication, numbers are employed to reveal patterns of social life. To see qualitative research as strictly disengaged from any form of counting is to miss the point that its basic strategy depends on the reconciliation of diverse research tactics.

It is our view that qualitative research can be performed as social science. Understanding the workings of a scientific endeavor, whether it is of the natural or social variety, entails an appreciation of its objectivity. By this convention, the objectivity of a piece of qualitative research is evaluated in terms of the reliability and validity of its observations—the two concepts to which this monograph is devoted.

Chapter 2 introduces the role of reliability and validity in the unfolding of science. Chapter 3 more fully explores the meaning of validity, and points out that much research (particularly nonqualitative research) lacks not only validity but also any means of appraising its validity. In Chapter 4, the history of qualitative research is seen as a cumulative effort to correct this flaw: Were it otherwise valueless, qualitative research would be justified solely as a validity check. Yet, as is pointed out in Chapter 5, much of the validity of qualitative research has been gained at the expense of reliability in the "discovery," or data-collection phase of research. Finally, Chapter 6 presents a model of the fieldwork activity that constitutes discovery in qualitative research, and provides some detailed instructions for maintaining reliability in the process.

2. RELIABILITY AND VALIDITY

Despite the prestige and success of natural science in recent years, application of science as a model for social "science" is not inevitable. Many have argued that social science has an intrinsically different set of goals that call for an altogether separate collection of methods. Others (nonscientists, it should be noted) contend that recent developments in the natural sciences entirely discredit the fundamental notions (such as objectivity) of an earlier and outdated science.

Yet, whatever their detailed goals, the natural and social sciences share an aspiration to cumulative collective knowledge that is of interest on its own merits to those other than the friends and admirers of its creators. This goal is exactly objectivity. In the natural sciences, objectivity is obtained in two ways. First, experience is reported in such a way that it is accessible to others, for example, when reporting an experiment every effort is made to describe the way the experiment was carried out, just in case somebody else would like to try the same thing. Second, the results of the experiment are reported in terms of theoretically meaningful variables, measured in ways that are themselves justifiable in terms of the relevant theories.

Since Wilhelm Dilthey and George Herbert Mead, the vast majority of social scientists have agreed that objectivity, in this sense, is an admirable goal. Yet, the description of reliability and validity ordinarily provided by nonqualitative social scientists rarely seems appropriate or relevant to the way in which qualitative researchers conduct their work.

It is the purpose of this book to reconcile the means-ends discrepancy. The remainder of this chapter will pursue the argument that, subject to clearly specifiable differences in goals and practice, social science is in every sense of the word fully as "scientific" as physics, and has fully as much need for reliability and validity as any other science.

The "Positivist" View

In recent decades, the social science literature has incorporated a great deal of discussion of an epistemology called "positivism." (The term is generally employed by those advocating some alternative view of knowledge, and often amounts to a straw man.) In its strongest form, positivism denies objectivity as defined here by assuming not only that there is an external world, but that the external world itself determines absolutely the one and only correct view that can be taken of it, independent of the process or circumstances of viewing. No one seriously defends such an ontology, but scholars attentive to the social and cultural construction of social things (including social science) point out that much research (particularly nonqualitative research) makes sense only in terms of a set of unexamined positivist assumptions.

Most often, these assumptions pertain to the "naturalness" of the measurement procedure employed. Thus a survey researcher may interview a large number of people about their political attitudes, and conclude that "public opinion" says something.

Such an assertion obviously concerns the investigator's theoretical view of the world as much as it does the psychic organization of the interviewees. The investigator's theory contains categories not imposed by the structure of empirical reality. Elements such as "attitudes" and "public opinion" serve rather to organize understanding of the world. Certainly, political and psychological theories that do not use these constructs (or even deny their meaningfulness) are possible, and treating analytic devices as though they are facts is the well-known fallacy of reification.

In response to the propensity of so many nonqualitative research traditions to use such hidden positivist assumptions, some social scientists have tended to overreact by stressing the possibility of alternative interpretations of everything to the exclusion of any effort to choose among them. This extreme relativism ignores the other side of objectivity—that there is an external world at all. It ignores the important distinction between knowledge and opinion, and results in everyone having a separate insight that cannot be reconciled with anyone else's.

Metaphysical polemics, often directed against caricatures of the opposing views, largely miss the point. As is shown in the next chapter, the problem is not so much one of metaphysics as it is a pragmatic question of the validity of measurements. The survey researcher who discusses attitudes is not wrong to do so. Rather, the researcher is wrong if he or she fails to acknowledge the theoretical basis on which it is meaningful to make measurements of such entities and to do so with survey questions addressed to a probability sample of voters.

For any observation (or measurement) to yield discovery, it must generate data that is (a) not already known and (b) identifiable as "new" by the theory already in place.[2] Most of the technology of "confirmatory" nonqualitative research in both the social and natural sciences is aimed at preventing discovery. When confirmatory research goes smoothly, everything comes out precisely as expected. Received theory is supported by one more example of its usefulness, and requires no change. As in everyday social life, confirmation is exactly the absence of insight.

In science, as in life, dramatic new discoveries must almost by definition be accidental ("serendipitous"). Indeed, they occur only in consequence of some kind of mistake.

The Discovery of the New

Henri Becquerel was studying the phenomenon of phosphorescence by exposing metal salts first to the sun and then to photographic plates. When the sky clouded over for an extended period, he tossed the uranium salts into a drawer with his photographic materials and knocked off work for a while (Badash, 1965). "*Merde! Je me suis planté!*" he must have muttered when he discovered that the film was ruined, but he was sufficiently prepared and alert to realize that he had discovered radioactivity.

More recently, the first men to hear the echo of the origin of the universe thought they were listening to guano. In 1964, Arno Penzias and Robert Wilson set out to measure the radio waves emitted from different latitudes in our disk-shaped galaxy. First, they had to identify what portions of the signal they received originated in the instrument itself. When they received a strong signal in microwave frequencies (where galaxies emit virtually no radiation), their first move was to devote considerable time and expense to cleaning out the "white dielectric material" deposited by pigeons in the antenna throat. This produced only a negligible decrease in signal strength (Penzias and Wilson, 1965). While Penzias and Wilson were in the antenna throat, Dicke et al. (1965) were proposing the hypothesis that traces of the high temperatures that occurred shortly after the (or a) "big bang" should still be observable, and predicting that they should sound very much like the signal heard by Penzias and Wilson. This "cosmic microwave radiation" is now considered the basic evidence for the truth of the "standard model" of the universe.

The history of the biomedical sciences, too, is full of examples of this particular kind of serendipity. Fleming (1946) discusses the irritation he felt when some kind of mold got into his staphylococcus culture and ruined the bacteria. He named the mold penicillin. Miller et al. (1955) inadvertently used a four-year-old bottle of DNA and discovered the hormonal element that provokes cell division in plants. Paul Ehrlich discovered the acid-fast method of staining tubercle bacilli only because he accidentally lit the stove on which his culture was resting; somewhat later, Hans Christian Joachim Gram accidentally grabbed the bottle of Lugol's iodine instead of the gentian violet, and only some of the bacteria (the "Gram-negative" ones) yielded up their purple color when he washed them off (Beveridge, 1950). And so on.

These historical examples illustrate how one feature of the hypothetico-deductive model of scientific progress is misleading: Hypothesis testing is not the only research activity in any scientific discipline. Indeed, the most dramatic discoveries necessarily come about some other way, because in order to test a hypothesis, the investigator must already know what it is he or she is going to discover.

The majority of nonqualitative methods in the social sciences are designed primarily for the logical testing of hypotheses.[3] Testing hypotheses is a useful, often essential element of research. It is also a useful model for the training of researchers, for it accustoms the novice to subject his or her predictions to the risk of empirical refutation.

As social scientists have come to recognize in recent decades, however, hypothesis testing is appropriate to only a small proportion of the questions they ask. Qualitative research has always retained the proper ideals of hypothesis-testing research— sound reasoning and the empirical risking of theory. But, in being intrinsically exploratory, it explicitly departs from certain strictures of the hypothetico-deductive model.

Formal logic, for instance, is not the only kind of sound reasoning. In fact, formal logic possesses certain flaws, such as its perverse insistence on the analytic "truth" of such statements as "everybody over twelve feet tall is named Fred," and "if Durkheim lives, then he is a rock star." (Formal logic is merely an arbitrary set of conventions. One of these conventions is that any false statement implies every other statement.) The prior explicit statement of hypotheses and null hypotheses is not the only way to subject predictions to empirical test. Each time Chauncey greets his old friend Ricky, he does expose himself to the unlikely possibility that he has mistaken a perfect stranger for Ricky. Much social research deliberately seeks out such "embarrassing" interaction; Agar (1982) has applied the hermeneutic term "breakdown" to these informative gaffes. The general commitment of qualitative researchers to interacting with their objects of study on the latter's home ground strongly encourages the discovery that what the researcher takes for granted at his home does not apply in the new situation. The anthropologist who returns alive from some exotic place must know something nontrivial about it.

Relaxing certain of the narrow definitions of the hypothetico-deductive model, then, facilitates discovery of the new and unexpected. It would be an error, however, to drop the scientific concern for objectivity. The scientific credo is one good way to permit the resolution of a conflict of opinion. It is not the only way; the scholastic solution, still prevalent in many disciplines called "humanities," relies on argument and rhetoric rather than on argument and demonstration. Another alternative is *argumentum ad imperium*—"might makes right." One attractive feature of the scientific solution is that it is an extension of the ordinary processes of inference that people use in everyday life (Piaget, 1954). As Wilhelm Dilthey pointed out, it is impossible to account for the observed reality of human interaction without acknowledging that human beings have an innate capacity to understand one another. Thus striving for ever-greater objectivity is as much a part of people's everyday social inference as it is of their everyday physical inference.

Components of Objectivity

The analogy between qualitative research and other scientific methods and traditions has its limitations. Yet the ability of practitioners of certain kinds of scientific endeavor to talk about what it is they do is much more advanced than that of qualitative researchers (Van Maanen, 1979). Indeed, a primary purpose of this monograph is to remedy that situation. It is often useful to examine methodological formulations from other traditions to assess their adaptability to qualitative research.

One appropriate and useful device first used in psychometrics (the field of tests and measurements) is the partitioning of objectivity into two components: *reliability* and *validity*. Loosely speaking, "reliability" is the extent to which a measurement procedure yields the same answer however and whenever it is carried out; "validity" is the extent to which it gives the correct answer.[4] These concepts apply equally well to qualitative observations.[5]

A standard physical example of reliability and validity involves the use of thermometers to measure temperature. A thermometer that shows the same reading of 82 degrees each time it is plunged into boiling water gives a reliable measurement. A second thermometer might give readings over a series of measurements that vary from around 100 degrees. The second thermometer would be unreliable but relatively valid, whereas the first would be invalid but perfectly reliable.

The standard example of the thermometer is neither very qualitative nor very familiar to social scientists. A rather homier (if artificial) example occurs when Chauncey sees a blond man across the room at a large cocktail party, and has the uncertain feeling that he knows him from somewhere. He looks again, sees the same thing, and continues to have the feelings of uncertainty. Chauncey has perfectly reliable data, and it is of no use. Is his feeling valid? (As in ordinary language, the technical use of the term "valid" is as a properly hedged weak synonym for "true.")

Chauncey might ask himself whether it seems he would know a person who looks like that, moves like that, dresses like that, and so on. Is the blond, in other words, apparently the sort of person Chauncey would know? Or he might ask himself subtler questions, such as whether people who look like that frequent the places he does. At a cocktail party, such a search for validity will probably fail because the guest list is deliberately socially homogeneous, and any two members are likely to have been in the same other places. So Chauncey must resort to empirical research if he is to discover whether his feeling is useful.

Perhaps Chauncey's least costly pilot project would be to ask the host what the blond man's name is, or whether in fact the host has relevant information (e.g., that the blond has just arrived in the country for the first time from a place Chauncey has never been, or that the three of them had a conversation last week). Another strategy would be to make ambiguous eye contact with the blond, in such a way as to assign to the other responsibility for acknowledging the acquaintance. Ultimately, it may prove necessary to confront him and ask, "Don't I know you?"

If Chauncey devotes as much time to worrying about his problem as it requires to read about it, we would conclude that he is socially inept, or at least painfully shy. This is one of the problems of methodological discussion: detailing the inferential steps in getting the job done looks picky and absurd. If we suppose this computation passes very quickly through Chauncey's mind as he gives the blond a second glance, we might better empathize with him. When discussing the validity checks of social research, it is useful to remember that a careful description of what is done generally tends to suggest an obsessive preoccupation with detail on the part of the researcher. This is an artifact of the fact of description, not a recommendation for compulsive behavior.

Objectivity, though the term has been taken by some to suggest a naive and inhumane version of vulgar positivism, is the essential basis of all good research. Without it, the only reason the reader of the research might have for accepting the conclusions of the investigator would be an authoritarian respect for the person of the author. Objectivity is the simultaneous realization of as much reliability and validity as possible. Reliability is the degree to which the finding is independent of accidental circumstances of the research, and validity is the degree to which the finding is interpreted in a correct way.

Reliability and validity are by no means symmetrical. It is easy to obtain perfect reliability with no validity at all (if, say, the thermometer is broken, or it is plunged into the wrong flask). Perfect validity, on the other hand, would assure perfect reliability, for every observation would yield the complete and exact truth.

As a means to the truth, social science has relied almost entirely on techniques for assuring reliability, in part because "perfect validity" is not even theoretically attainable. Most nonqualitative research methodologies come complete with a variety of checks on reliability, and none on validity.

3. THE PROBLEM OF VALIDITY

No experiment can be perfectly controlled, and no measuring instrument can be perfectly calibrated. All measurement, therefore, is to some degree suspect. When the measurement is nonqualitative, this reservation may amount to no more than the acknowledgment that "accuracy" is limited.[6] More generally, however, the issue of validity is a fundamental problem of theory.

To discuss the validity of a thermometer reading, a physical theory is necessary. The theory must posit not only that mercury expands linearly with temperature, but that water in fact boils at 100°. With such a theory, a thermometer that reads 82° when the water breaks into a boil can be reckoned inaccurate. Yet if the theory asserts that water boils at different temperatures under different ambient pressures, the same measurement may be valid under different circumstances—say, at one-half an atmosphere. In the case of qualitative observations, the issue of validity is not a matter of methodological hair-splitting about the fifth decimal point, but a question of whether the researcher sees what he or she thinks he or she sees.

In the real world, validity is the issue of much contention over the organization of actions and events. In the scientific world, validity is a common denomination in cause and effect discussions of "pragmatic utility," "fruitfulness," "felicity of notation," and "spuriousness." (These terms correspond to the terms "generality of scope," "robustness," "replicability," and "insignificance" applied to the sister issue of reliability in more abstract contexts.)

To focus on the validity of an observation or an instrument is to care about whether measurements have currency (what do the observations buy?), and about whether phenomena are properly labeled (what are the right names for variables?). The notions of *apparent validity, instrumental validity,* and *theoretical validity* are helpful in addressing these problems.

In the best of worlds, a measuring instrument is so closely linked to the phenomena under observation that it is "obviously" providing valid data. Formal examinations of competence and achievement (e.g., academic, civil service, professional tests) are based on this kind of apparent validity: correct answers are preferred to incorrect ones. Unfortunately, the validity of measurements is too seldom evident "on the face of things." Conclusions of apparent validity are not entirely out of order, but they can be illusory. Apparent validity suggests or assumes instrumental or theoretical validity; it can exist without them.

A measurement procedure is said to have instrumental validity (also referred to as "pragmatic" and "criterion" validity) if it can be shown that observations match those generated by an alternative procedure that is itself accepted as valid. In most practical applications, demonstrating the validity of a measurement against a criterion is essentially unproblematic (Nunnally, 1959). The expansion of a column of mercury can be shown to correspond to other criteria of temperature such as vapor pressure or electrical conductivity ("concurrent validity"); scores on the Graduate Record Examinations correlate with the success of candidates in school and in their profession ("predictive validity"). The distinction between apparent and instrumental validity can be illustrated by imagining a Graduate Record Examination on which those students who do well in graduate school get all the questions wrong, whereas those who do poorly in graduate school answer many of them correctly. For the instrumental purpose of selecting graduate students, such an exam might be excellent, but since it would have no apparent validity, it would doubtless be illegal.

Finally, measurement procedures are seen to exhibit theoretical validity ("construct validity") if there is substantial evidence that the theoretical paradigm rightly corresponds to observations (Cronbach and Meehl, 1955). For example, if the construct "anomie" is taken as the subjective cultural state that associates sudden disruptions of the environment with an increase in deviant behavior (Durkheim, 1951), giving the same name to a measurement of feelings of powerlessness (Srole, 1956) can be questioned—unless feelings of powerlessness can be independently shown related both to environmental disruption and to deviant behavior.[7] Theoretical validity is a hedge against concepts that are virtually defined as puns. For example, those who refer to an employer's furnishing tools to his or her workers as "alienation" from the tools of production beg the crucial theoretical question of whether that arrangement inevitably produces negative feelings on the part of the worker.

Theoretical validity underlies discussions of both apparent and instrumental validity. If the perverse examination on which good students differentially give the wrong answers were backed by a theoretical reason why it worked, its use could be justified without resorting to apparent validity. Thermometers are not ordinarily calibrated by comparison with a standard thermometer kept in the Bureau of Standards. Instead, they are calibrated by direct reference to the "boiling point of water"—a notion heavily burdened with a theory that says that under controlled circumstances water boils at a constant temperature.

Calling Things by the Right Names

Of course, definitions are made by people, and can be made any way the definer chooses. Consider this well-known exchange:

"There's glory for you!"

"I don't know what you mean by 'glory,' " Alice said.

Humpty Dumpty smiled contemptuously. "Of course you don't—till I tell you. I meant, 'there's a nice knock-down argument.' "

"But 'glory' doesn't mean 'a nice knock-down argument,' " Alice objected.

"When I use a word," Humpty Dumpty said, in rather a scornful tone, "it means just what I choose it to mean—neither more nor less."

"The question is," said Alice, "whether you can make words mean so many different things."

"The question is," said Humpty Dumpty, "which is to be master, that's all" [Lewis Carroll, 1960: 268-269].

In fact, Dodgson (Lewis Carroll) took a strongly nominalist position on the issue of definitions, arguing (according to Gardner, in Carroll, 1960) that if a writer chooses to produce a whole book in which "black" means white and the reverse, it is the responsibility of the reader to adapt. Yet a definition that violates the associations given a familiar term by theory or by ordinary language is useful only as Veblenian irony.[8] Goldschmidt (1982: 642), arguing against the use of the same term for voluntary human behavior and some other behavior on the part of another species, puts it in the following way:

> The very fact that terms must be supplied with arbitrary meanings requires that words be used with a great sense of responsibility. This responsibility is twofold: first, to established usage; second, to the limitations that the definitions selected impose on the user.

In other words, we are under considerable constraint to keep our thinking clear by calling things by their right names. Graff (1979: 90), calling down relativistic "deconstructionist" literary critics who disparage any concern for validity on the grounds that external reality is just a matter of opinion, emphasizes that

> our ability to identify a perverse use of terms as perverse depends on the assumption that there is such a thing as calling things by their right names, and this in turn depends on the assumption that there is a common world and that language's relation to it is not wholly arbitrary.

Three Illustrations

Questions concerning all three kinds of validity—apparent validity, instrumental validity, and theoretical validity—arise in ethnographic field research. Apparent validity can be chimerical, and may not signify theoretical validity. Instrumental validity is ultimately circular, and cannot assure theoretical validity unless the criterion itself is theoretically valid. Theoretical validity, unfortunately, is difficult to determine by methods other than qualitative research. Testing hypotheses against explicit alternatives cannot guard against unanticipated sources of invalidity. The fieldworker, on the other hand, is continuously engaged in something very like hypothesis testing, but that effectively checks perception and understanding against the whole range of possible sources of error. He or she draws tentative conclusions from his or her current understanding of the situation as a whole, and acts upon them. Where, for unanticipated reasons, this understanding is invalid, the qualitative researcher will sooner or later (often to the researcher's intense dismay) find out about it.

Three examples illustrate some of the pitfalls in unthinking acceptance of apparently valid data. The first shows the difference between reliability and validity. The second and third come from the literature of nonqualitative research, and in different ways display the relative disadvantage under which experimental and survey researchers labor.

"WHEN DO YOU GIVE COCA TO ANIMALS?"

In 1976, we jointly conducted field research in several South American countries with the goal of understanding prevailing cognitions and usages of coca, the organic source of the alkaloid cocaine. Part of this work focused on the coca knowledge of the Peruvian urban lower-middle class, as exemplified by taxi drivers, merchants, and restaurant personnel (all cosmopolitan and accessible roles).

In modern Peru, coca is perhaps less centrally located within the cultural milieu of Quechua-speaking *indios* and *mestizos* than it was in the postconquest era, but coca is emphatically not a predominantly displayed element of non-Indian life. Nonetheless, coca is widely available and legal throughout the country. At the outset, we were acquainted with the social problems of coca as they were identified by the Peruvian government and the tourist brochures. The twin foci were a notoriously successful illicit cocaine industry, and the persistence of traditional Quechua reliance on coca leaves.

We proceeded by engaging the range of urban Peruvians at our disposal in informal conversation about coca. As it turned out, our Mexican Spanish was sufficient to explore a domain loaded with ambiguity. (We were able to communicate that we cared about native attitudes toward a plant, and not about obtaining drugs.)

Our research approach was typified by a noncommittal question of the following general order: "¿Y la coca?" (Tell us about coca!") This elicited a highly uniform, but limited, set of coca beliefs and practices. We discovered everything that we had already read about. Coca was, for example, considered to be a dirty Quechua vice. And, as advertised in the airline pamphlets, coca tea was suitable for allaying altitude sickness experienced by tourists.

In time, we became uncomfortable with the sameness of answers to our coca questions.[9] In a sense, our measurement was excessively reliable! The saccharin compatibility between what we were told and what we knew to be the received view of coca forced us to reconsider our method.

We decided to try a new tack. So we tried apparently less sensible questions, such as "¿Cúanda da Ud. la coca a los animales?" ("When do you give coca to animals?") and "Como averiguó Ud. que no le gusta la coca?" ("How did you find out you don't like coca?"). Surprisingly, these "silly" questions worked. Our bemused informants began to open up and elaborate on their personal, if modest, commitments to coca. As a result, we learned that most Peruvian ladinos had a fairly elaborate knowledge of the merits and demerits of coca, and most had some first-hand experience. Coca was a broad-spectrum anti-inflammatory, a stimulant, a hunger and thirst depressant, part of the Quechua costume, and so forth.

This account of coca is an abbreviation of some field research moments in South America. It is not a tale of overcoming a problem with rapport. Rather, it illustrates that the reliability of the observations did not entail theoretical validity. Plainly, the original question had yielded responses to stimuli the investigators had underestimated (for example, the social environment of the interaction). The informants had smoothly slipped the punch of the feeble first question. Only with an outrageous second strategy did the researchers manage to initiate a productive exchange.

GENDER AND CONFORMITY

Beginning in the mid-1950s, a body of social psychology literature accumulated that led to the conclusion that women are more intrinsically "conformist" than men (e.g., Crutchfield, 1955; Janis and Field, 1959). Subsequently, and until very recently, handbooks and textbooks typically reported this finding as an accomplished fact. Freedman et al. (1970: 239, quoted in Eagly, 1978: 86), for example, note the following:

> The most consistent and strongest factor that differentiates people in the amount they conform is their sex. Women conform more than men. . . . This difference between men and women has been found in virtually every study in which both sexes participated.

In the 1970s Maccoby and Jacklin (1974) and Eagly (1978) reviewed this literature and concluded that the central "finding" was essentially illusory. Eagly, for example, examined 144 separate studies that attended to the issue, and found evidence that females conform more than males in only 32 (22 percent) of them. (Several others found that males conform more than females.) Furthermore, Eagly adduced some reasons for the exposed inconsistency in the literature. Among them she noted that those studies that showed females more conformist utilized politicoeconomic arguments or spatial judgments as the stimulus. Because women are less involved in such stimuli than are men, and less confident of their own initial judgments, it is easy to suppose that under those circumstances they would be more likely to yield their own judgments to those of others.

Sistrunk and McDavid (1971) had by that time found that, whereas women did conform to the judgments of male peers about specialized tools, men yielded to women's judgments about needlework, and there was no difference between the sexes in conformity to others' judgments about rock stars. Goldberg (1974) found that the same essay attributed to a man was given more credence by a female audience than if attributed to a woman, unless the subject of the paper was education or nutrition; in these so-called women's fields, attribution to a woman increased the credibility of the argument. Eagly explained the reluctance of her profession to look impartially at the facts in this way: It is "obvious" that women conform more than men, and those studies supporting this common-sense view are the ones that tend to be cited and believed. Evidently, social psychologists, like all people, are not immune to what Ross et al. (1976) call the "fundamental attribution error": explaining others' behavior on the grounds of personal disposition to behave in such ways across a variety of situations, rather than (as we interpret our own behavior) as a response to circumstantial and contextual pressures.

The error made in the early studies of gender and conformity was an error of theoretical validity. Clearly, many of the studies measured not conformity but the variable of familiarity with stimuli. A proper conclusion would have been that women had less interest in and familiarity with spatial judgments and politicoeconomic issues than men. Unfortunately, the variable was given the wrong label, and the spurious, but socially acceptable, conclusion (that women in general have less courage of their convictions) was drawn.

THE DISTRIBUTION OF WEALTH IN SRI LANKA

Leach (1967) has presented a classical critique of a social survey (Sarkar and Tambiah, 1957) that, according to Leach, reached all the wrong conclusions about the distribution of wealth in a part of Sri Lanka. The survey, for example, defined a "household" as "persons who cook their rice from the same pot." By this definition, they found the striking statistic that some 66 percent of households owned no paddy land. Leach points out from his field experience in a culturally similar nearby village that it is very common for a young married couple to live in the compound of the husband's father and work the land that is the husband's own in all but formal title. As every married woman has her own cooking pot, such a couple would be considered "landless," independent of the size or value of the holdings the husband manages and expects to inherit. Indeed, such a son's relationship would be called *anda* (sharecropping). The frequency of anda was seen by Tambiah et al. to reflect unequal land distribution and contribute to the disintegration of the village.

Tambiah and his co-workers also noted the remarkable difference in yield of the land held by rich and poor members of the community. Leach points out that wealthier landowners generally own the lands developed since purchase from the crown around the turn of the century, whereas less prosperous land-holders are more likely to own older lands measured by tradi-tional methods. He also points out that the standardized con-version factor used by the social surveyors to render the size of traditional plots in acres was wrong. This factor systematically overestimates the size of traditional plots by 50 percent. Un-critical acceptance of these nonsensical "acreage" figures ap-parently led the Tambiah team to conclude that the traditional land was unproductive because it yielded less per "acre."

Leach's objection follows directly from a sensitivity to theo-retical validity. He points out merely that the survey researcher (who Leach labels "the sociologist") often does not really know what his or her variables are, and so risks entirely invalid inferences:

> What impresses me here is that when the sociologists encounter an unexpected discrepancy of this sort they accept the validity of their questionnaire data and simply analyse the figures so as to discover their statistical significance. In contrast, the anthropologist sus-pects the validity of the original data as such and looks for a source of error [Leach, 1967: 81].

Leach was able to display these insights so easily because he had previously done qualitative field research in a nearby, culturally similar area. Even when the quantitative reliability of survey research is essential to the research goal, the additional perspective of qualitative research is useful as a rule for the purpose of assuring validity.

Field Research as a Validity Check

Believing a principle to be true when it is not (i.e., mistakenly "rejecting the null hypothesis") is called "type one error." It is not the only possible kind. "Type two error" is rejecting a principle when in fact it is true. "Type three error" is asking the wrong question (Raiffa, 1968, credits John Tukey with this insight.) Asking the wrong question actually is the source of most validity errors. Devices to guard against asking the wrong question are critically important to the researcher.

Diversity of method is a strong candidate for such a device. Webb et al. (1966: 174) advocate this kind of (theoretical) validity check:

> The most fertile search for validity comes from a combined series of difference measures, each with its idiosyncratic weaknesses, each pointed to a single hypothesis. When a hypothesis can survive the confrontation of a series of complementary methods of testing, it contains a degree of validity unattainable by one tested within the more constricted framework of a single method.

Webb et al. agree, in other words, with the moral we draw from the three war stories above—that the various errors were avoidable by multiple exposures of differing kinds to the problem area. It is also true that the more diffuse and less focused the method, the wider net it casts. This, too, is a basic argument for the value of qualitative research.

Typically, the qualitative researcher arrives on the scene with considerable theoretical baggage but very little idea of what will happen next. Using theory, common sense, and any resources at hand, the researcher attempts first, to survive in the field situation, and second, to work him- or herself into a position where both observation and interviewing of locals will be possible.

Face-to-face, routine contact with people continues throughout the period of fieldwork, and unless the fieldworker is unusually craven or complacent, his or her emerging hypotheses are continually tested in stronger and stronger ways in the pragmatic routine of everyday life. This "method" is unusually sensitive to discrepancies between the meanings presumed by investigators and those understood by the target population. Indeed, this is one reason that qualitative research has been such a dominant method in the anthropological study of exotic populations, where it is quite apparent that the investigator makes assumptions about meanings, situations, and attributions at his or her own risk. Because of this built-in sensitivity, field research intrinsically possesses certain kinds of validities not ordinarily possessed by nonqualitative methods.

The "automatic" validity of qualitative field research has contributed to the romantic image of the anthropologist struggling to survive under maximally difficult social and physical circumstances. Anthropologists do not struggle alone. The historical record, outlined in the next chapter, indicates that a high proportion of field research technique has been developed in the streets of Chicago and other urban and industrial contexts by people who called themselves sociologists (and sometimes political scientists or social psychologists). Nonetheless, simply by virtue of being "in the field"—in territory controlled by the investigatees rather than the investigator—qualitative research partakes of this virtue of adversity.

To the extent that confirmatory methods are used, they are used quickly and informally, rather than constituting entire research projects of themselves, and they belong to the data-collection rather than the analysis phase of the research. The field investigator simply does not have the resources to "control all relevant variables"; when he or she takes time out for statistical analysis, the researcher's tools are essentially restricted to those that can be written on the back of an envelope. Above all, the field researcher is at the mercy of the world view of his or her subjects.

This is not to take an entirely idealist view. Very often, the determining factor in human life is material reality. The ratio of population to available food resources in a particular time and place, for example, is an ecological fact with immense consequences for the organization of everyday life and thought. As Harris (1979) points out, cultures that do not somehow manage to adapt the cognitive structures of their members to the physical environment do not last long.

Yet the study of human groups and cultures must take members' meanings into account. First, social evolution of whatever sort is a very slow process compared with environmental change. Even in the large-scale examples of human evolution that concern some anthropologists, emplaced cognitive structures have substantial effects in two ways. It takes generations for certain kinds of cultural entities to change noticeably, and it is a truism that for the individual in the short run, behavior is governed by norms, beliefs, and expectations. It is also true that the measurement of material reality is often intrinsically problematic, particularly when some interaction with subjects is necessary. It may be relatively easy, in practically any culture, to count the number of people living in a village. But the demographer may need other information, such as the number of live births over some period of time. It is typical of field demographers' experience around the world that this information is difficult to elicit with straightforward questions. Having large numbers of children often has positive (or negative) status connotations, so that members are motivated, even when they are trying to be honest, to miscount. Often it is difficult to elicit an exhaustive list of the children a woman has ever had, because after the enumeration is complete it turns out that, oh yes, there was another one, but it broke.

We have no other technology for making this kind of validity check than long-run personal interaction. We can never be absolutely sure that we understand all the idiosyncratic cultural implications of anything, but the sensitive, intelligent fieldworker armed with a good theoretical orientation and good rapport over a long period of time is the best check we can make.

4. TOWARD THEORETICAL VALIDITY

Qualitative research finds its formal and intertwined roots in the traditions of cultural anthropology and American sociology. Implicitly oriented to the question of validity, generations of field researchers have for over a hundred years worked and reworked the particulars of ethnographic inquiry. This has involved several important breakthroughs in method. In a generic way, these refinements on the work of the earliest of researchers are particularly associated with the contributions of Franz Boas, Bronislaw Malinowski, and Robert Park.[10]

The Ancestors

Most cultures probably define a role that includes anthropology (or more properly, *xenology*, the study of foreigners). We have records of ethnographic fieldwork in the European tradition dating at least to the unsung sources of Herodotus of Helicarnassus (c. 484-425 B.C.). In 1800, Joseph-Marie Dégerando, a member of the pioneering *Société des Observateurs de l'Homme*, published a field manual for a scientific expedition, remarking,

> The first fault that we notice in the observations of explorers on savages is their incompleteness; it was only to be expected, given the shortness of their stay, the division of their attention, and the absence of any regular tabulation of their findings [Degérando, 1969: 65].[11]

In 1843, Gustave Klemm published a compilation of data on other cultures comparable in intent to Murdock's (1967) *Ethnographic Atlas*. These data were collected in large part by means of watching and interviewing native peoples, often in their natural environment. Among Klemm's sources were Ynca Garcilaso de la Vega's Peruvian history, Joseph Banks' observations in Polynesia from Captain James Cook's 1768-1781 voyages, and Henry Rowe Schoolcraft's reports of decades spent among the Algonquians. Also in 1843, the Royal Anthropological Institute of Great Britain and Ireland commissioned J. C. Prichard to chair a committee that compiled a field guide (*Notes and Queries on Anthropology*, first edition, 1874) for those engaged in collecting primary data.

In the meantime, the evolutionary theories of Charles Lyell, Herbert Spencer, and Charles Darwin had laid sufficient groundwork for the consolidation of a professional role by Lewis Henry Morgan (1818-1881), Edward B. Tylor (1832-1917), and Sir James G. Frazer (1854-1941).[12] These "founding fathers" of anthropology compiled, transcribed, and evaluated the reports of colonial officials, missionaries, merchants, and others who had described and commented upon the customs and culture of non-Western societies.

Contemporary anthropologists react with a certain ambivalence to the achievements of these men. On the one hand, their contributions to the theory of social evolution, to the "comparative method," and to accurate knowledge of the substantive details of cultural variation are gigantic. Further, there is a record of considerable intercultural travel, dabbling, and casual mixing with the natives, though only Morgan seems to have spent any considerable time actually interacting with members of other cultures. On the other hand, modern anthropologists are not willing to dignify what these figures did with the respectful term "fieldwork." As Evans-Pritchard (1951: 71-72) insists,

> It is indeed surprising that, with the exception of Morgan's study of the Iroquois . . . not a single anthropologist conducted field studies till the end of the nineteenth century. . . . Williams James tells us that when he asked Sir James Frazer about natives he had known, Frazer exclaimed, "But heaven forbid!"[13]

We are left with rather a paradox. Although in the iconography of both sociology and anthropology the discipline of anthropology (and implicitly the technology of qualitative research) grew "from nothing to maturity" in the period 1860-1890 (Tax, 1955), its legendary practitioners at that time obviously failed to match the quality of the field research of nonprofessionals centuries earlier.[14]

This paradox is resolved when we recognize that these practitioners of "verandah" (or "armchair") anthropology did part of the job extraordinarily well. Their sin of omission, by contemporary standards, was to do exclusively secondary analysis, and to lack any commitment to the fieldwork experience. The kind of work they did would today be seen as a reasonable model for a student paper, such as a "library research" master's thesis, rather than for genuinely "professional" work.[15]

Papa Franz

Much of what was called "social anthropology" in Britain was called "sociology" on the continent, and it was under this latter name that it was first taught in the United States, notably at the new universities of Johns Hopkins and Chicago. William G. Sumner taught a course in sociology at Yale in 1876, and by 1889 the University of Kansas, seeking a trained sociologist, solicited F. W. Blackmar from the well-known program at the Hopkins. In 1892, the new University of Chicago opened with a department of "social science and anthropology" consisting of sociologists Albion Small and C. W. Henderson (Small, 1916).

The term "anthropology" continued to carry a certain implication of gentlemanly amateurism until 1896, when Franz Boas, armed with a German doctorate in physics and field experience in Greenland, came to Columbia University (where Franklin Giddings had been teaching sociology for some years). At Columbia, Boas established the profession of cultural anthropology that he was to dominate for the rest of his life.[16] His mission, according to Harris (1968), was "to rid anthropology of its amateurs and armchair specialists" by making ethnographic research in the field the central experience and minimum attribute of professional status. To the present day, "field experience" constitutes such an attribute for anthropology, and the implicit requirement of fieldwork virtually suffices to distinguish the anthropologist from the sociologist.[17]

Both as a charismatic teacher and as a collector of ethnographic materials, Boas was tireless. Virtually every major anthropologist working in the United States during the first half of the century was trained, directly or indirectly, by Boas, and every professional organization in the discipline felt his impact.

Boas was revolted by the wildly speculative and amateurish pronouncements that passed at the time for anthropology, and was equally offended by the crude racism into whose service these "theories" were typically pressed. In response, Boas insisted not only that the analyst collect his or her own data, but that it be reported as nearly without comment or interpretation as possible.

Clearly, he overdid it. Boas in effect discarded the possibility of any sort of explicit theory. He seems not to have realized that a thousand pages of Kwakiutl routines and recipes do not, by themselves, produce understandings of a culture. Not only did Boas fail to produce a single overall description of any culture during his long career, he did not even organize his thousands of pages of materials in such a way that anyone else has ever been able to summarize them. Shortly after Boas's death, Murdock (1949: xiv) characterized him critically as

> extravagantly overrated by his disciples . . . the most unsystematic of theorists, his numerous kernels of genuine insight being scattered amongst much pedantic chaff. He was not even a good field worker [and in a footnote]. Despite Boas' "five-foot-shelf" of monographs on the Kwakiutl, this tribe falls into the quartile of those whose social structure and related practices are least adequately described among the 250 covered in the present study.

Murdock's strong statement has been disputed, but it is certain that Boas's fieldwork was by contemporary standards inadequate in a number of respects. He seems never to have spent more than a few weeks in any one field site, and his data are devoid of any detailed observation or interviewing. Nor did he successfully communicate the qualitative techniques at which he was expert to his students. Mead (1972: 151-152) remarks, "I really did not know much about fieldwork. The course on methods that Professor Boas taught was not about fieldwork. It was about theory—how material could be organized to support or call in question some theoretical point."

It is patently unfair, however, to judge the man who single-handedly created and disseminated the "ethos" of fieldwork for failing to match the standards that later developed largely out of his own work. A more appropriate criticism would be that Boas and his students, fundamentally unsympathetic to theory of any kind, rarely supported any theoretical point, but exclusively employed their evidence to call in question those of others. In rejecting "bad" theory, Boas neglected to replace it with good theory.

Malinowski

At the outbreak of World War I, a young Polish anthropologist named Bronislaw Malinowski was arrested in Australia as an enemy alien and confined to the South Pacific by the British. Upon his return to England, he published several monographs about the lives of the Trobriand Islanders that have remained exemplars of what anthropological fieldwork can do. Reading Malinowski's reports gives insight into the life of a foreign people that makes them seem people like ourselves doing their best under ecological and historical circumstances different from ours, rather than incomprehensibly savage primitives. For many, Malinowski has represented the ethnographer as hero—the outstanding individual with the courage to move alone into a "savage" village and the perceptiveness to understand and explain what the people of that village were up to (Sontag, 1963).

The posthumous publication of Malinowski's *Diary In The Strict Sense Of The Term* in 1967 came as a rude shock to the profession. The *Diary*, never intended for publication, reveals Malinowski as a bitchy, neurotic, and self-centered individual (though one who in these pages is capable of considerable candor). This revelation compromises not the credibility or quality of Malinowski's professional achievement but the myth that good field research arises from the saintlike sympathy of an extraordinary virtuoso of humanity. Geertz (1974: 27) has perceptively analyzed the insight we obtain from the *Diary*:

> If anthropological understanding does not stem, as we have been taught to believe, from some sort of extraordinary sensibility, an almost preternatural capacity to think, feel, and perceive like a native (a word, I should hurry to say, I use here "in the strict sense of the term"), then how is anthropological knowledge of the way natives think, feel, and perceive possible?

Geertz was correct in taking the scandalized response of the profession to the publication of the *Diary* as evidence that field researchers have been emulating a myth. Apparently, Malinowski did not himself employ the methods his talented and worshipful students tried to copy (and very nearly succeeded in inventing). He did not respect (or even like) the Trobrianders—or apparently much of anybody else. Rather than having a special gift of sympathy that enabled him to transcend cultural differences, he appears to have been obsessively self-involved (at least during his stay in the Trobriand Islands).

What the best ethnographers have achieved, then, is to represent the natives' way of making sense of their experience in a language that transcends the culture-specific experience of the world of either the natives or the readers. Such a language would be an "etic," or "experience-distant" language. For Geertz's own "interpretive" work, the experience-distant categories are not explicitly described. They are hermeneutically suggested by

> the most local of local detail and the most global of global structure . . . the sort of exotic minutiae (lexical antitheses, categorical schemes, morphophonemic transformations) that make even the best ethnographies a trial to read and the sort of sweeping generalizations ("quietism," "dramatism," "contextual-ism") that makes all but the most pedestrian of them somewhat implausible [Geertz, 1974: 43].

Much of what is described as "interpretive" ethnography deliberately employs concepts not so very distant from the experience of its intended readership. Unlike Malinowski's work, this product gains its eminent readability (and its popularity with those who have not devoted themselves to a technical study of theoretical terms) at the expense of a certain ad hoc quality, and difficulty in making generalizations that apply to other ethnographic situations. Other ethnographers tie their interpretation to well-developed and often difficult theoretical schemes, as Malinowski employed psychoanalytic theory, and as some currently propose mathematical models.

The Chicago School

While Boas and Malinowski were staffing the discipline of anthropology, another charismatic figure, Robert E. Park, at Chicago, was training a generation of ethnographic fieldworkers who called themselves sociologists in a department that was by his arrival in 1913 called "sociology and anthropology." Pursuing the characteristically American blend of German theory and urban reform orientation encouraged by Small and W. I. Thomas at Chicago, Park's students and junior colleagues published dozens of books and monographs during the 1920s and 1930s based on ethnographic research in the city.[18]

Park initiated a special camaraderie at Chicago. Outside the classroom, he recruited faculty, graduate students, and alumni to partake in the monthly Evening Meetings of the Society for Social Research, a sort of "sociological society in miniature" (Blumer, 1983). Further, Park sustained the interest of field researchers in the network who resided outside of Chicago with the Society's *Bulletin*, and also with summer workshops he organized with Ernest W. Burgess.

Inside the classroom, Park brought sophistication to Chicago in two areas that proved critical for the development of "participant observation," or ethnographic sociology: a knowledge of the principles of what was then called "natural history" (and would now be called environmental biology), and a dozen years' experience as a newspaper reporter and city editor. He was thoroughly familiar with the work of Boas and Malinowski, and was in fact the guiding impulse behind the hiring of many of their students in the Department of Sociology. (One of Boas's students, Fay Cooper-Cole, became the first chairperson of a separate Department of Anthropology in 1929.)

Initially, at least, the Chicago School emphasized certain values and assumptions about the social world that differed from those stressed by fieldworkers in remote and exotic places. Park shared with the other major figures of the Chicago School a passionate concern for the mystique of the city as a dense, heterogeneous, conflictful, and very exciting place.[19] In conjunction with the newspaper reporter's commitment to meeting deadlines and breaking stories, this added a dimension to field research as identified with Malinowski.

Park literally forced his students from the library to the streets (Emerson, 1983). Although this strategy contributed to the vigor of Chicago students, Park's enthusiasm at getting studies accomplished in a socially responsible and timely manner concealed a neglect of any standardization of method. As perhaps sociology's original participant observer, Nels Anderson (1961) revealed later, "the only instruction I recall from Park was, 'Write down only what you see, hear, and know, like a newspaper reporter.' "[20]

Douglas (1976) goes so far as to assert that Park's inclination toward cultural anthropology ultimately diluted the contribution he was able to make toward "investigative" styles of research. In comparing a 1928 field research manual by Vivien Palmer with Buford Junker's 1960 manual (both from the Chicago School), Douglas notes that the 1928 manuscript "contains no significant reference to anthropology," while Junker "uses anthropological and sociological sources indiscriminately." At the same time, Douglas finds newer sociological work lacking in the suspicious, exposé-seeking investigative intent he feels Park's journalistic background brought to the work of the Chicago School in its heyday. Douglas attributes the loss of the "conflict model" largely to the influence of anthropologists recruited by Park such as Robert Redfield and W. Lloyd Warner. Douglas's statement is rather strong, and certainly exaggerates the insensitivity of anthropologists to diversity and conflict even in small, non-Western communities. Whether or not Park was able to sustain as aggressive a skeptical position as a muckraker would want, Douglas properly emphasizes the power of the journalistic ideals that nourished Park's Chicago School.

Stages and Phases

Obviously, Frazer, Boas, Malinowski, and Park were each more skilled at certain aspects, or phases, of the qualitative research process than at others. Yet, while their careers largely overlapped, it is clear that they built on one another's achievements in much the same order as the sequence of phases of a particular research project. Boas's emphasis on accurate collection of data presupposes (perhaps wrongly, in Boas's case) sufficient theoretical orientation to know what data is important.

Malinowski's analysis and interpretation certainly presupposes good data—which for Malinowski required immense investment of time in the field to collect. And even as a city editor, Park demanded accurate data and adequate analysis prior to writing a story.

Each of these three advances over the earliest professional ethnography has improved our confidence in the validity of our work. Yet the tradition of qualitative research that has been outlined here has grown up almost independently of the more quantitative research methods (such as experiments and social surveys) that have emphasized the issue of reliability.

5. THE PROBLEM OF RELIABILITY

Comparison of findings is a basic process of scientific, as well as everyday life. Knowing what conclusions to draw when findings differ across studies (or even when they agree) depends upon evaluations of the validity (see Chapter 3) and reliability of observations.

Observations entail the recording of the reaction of some entity to some stimulus, even if the only stimulus is the act of measurement. Reliability depends essentially on explicitly described observational procedures. It is useful to distinguish several kinds of reliability. These are *quixotic reliability, diachronic reliability,* and *synchronic reliability.*

"Quixotic reliability" refers to the circumstances in which a single method of observation continually yields an unvarying measurement.[21] The problem with reliability of this sort is that it is trivial and misleading. The absurd case of the broken thermometer is an instance of this kind of reliability. In ethnographic research, quixotic reliability frequently proves only that the investigator has managed to observe or elicit "party line" or rehearsed information. Americans, for example, reliably respond to the question, "How are you?" with the knee-jerk "Fine." The reliability of this answer does not make it useful data about how Americans are.

"Diachronic reliability" refers to the stability of an observation through time. In the social sciences, the concept is manifest in test-retest paradigms of experimental psychology and survey research. Diachronic reliability is conventionally demonstrated by similarity of measurements, or findings, taken at different times. The general applicability of diachronic reliability is somewhat diminished by the fact that it is only appropriate to measurements of features and entities that remain unchanged in a changing world. In the study of sociocultural phenomena, it is often dangerous to assume that configurations of data would be isomorphic across substantial intervals of time. To make such an assumption is to deny history.

"Synchronic reliability" refers to the similarity of observations within the same time period. Unlike quixotic reliability, synchronic reliability rarely involves identical observations, but rather observations that are consistent with respect to the particular features of interest to the observer. In the apocryphal story of the Tower of Pisa, Galileo's observation that unlike objects took the same length of time to reach the ground was reliable despite the unlikeness of the objects. This kind of internal reliability can be evaluated by comparisons of data elicited by alternate forms (e.g., split-half testing, interrater correlation). Paradoxically, synchronic reliability can be most useful to field researchers when it fails because a disconfirmation of synchronic reliability forces the ethnographer to imagine how multiple, but somehow different, qualitative measurements might simultaneously be true.

The main thrust of methodological development in qualitative research during the last century has been toward greater validity. In contrast to the concerns of many nonqualitative traditions, issues of reliability have received little attention. The following illustrations from qualitative research concern trade-offs in attaining kinds of reliability, and also hint again at the delicate links between reliability and validity issues.

Three Illustrations

COMMUNITY POWER STRUCTURE

Hunter's (1953) description of the workings of oligarchic authority in "Regional City" (Atlanta) went somewhat beyond the sociological/anthropological tradition of community studies typified by the Lynds' (1929) study of "Middletown" (Muncie) and Warner's (1941) "Yankee City" (Newburyport) series. Hunter (1953: 233) concluded that power in Atlanta is demonstrably in the hands of a small clique whose

> leaders are interested in maintaining their own positions which give them such things as wealth, power, and prestige. They are fearful that any swaying of the balance of power may destroy the positions they now hold, and of course they could be right, although it is felt that a case could be made for allaying their fears.

Hunter's study received a good deal of praise, but it also provoked a number of rather irritable attacks from both outraged residents of Atlanta and social scientists, particularly political scientists. These disagreements culminated in an elaborate study of the political workings of New Haven (Dahl, 1961) that reached a very different conclusion. Dahl found no single group in New Haven with overwhelming power, though the dynamic and popular mayor occupied a central position as "chief negotiator."

Because the studies were done in different cities at different times, the difference in their findings could be attributed either to diachronic or synchronic unreliability—that is, to the simple fact that the workings of power were different in Dahl's New Haven and Hunter's Atlanta. But while the partisans of both Hunter and Dahl would probably be willing to stipulate such a difference, they agree that the main reason for the difference in results was a difference in method. Hunter obtained lists of prominent individuals, and employed a panel of judges to select from the lists those who were "most influential." The people on this short list were then interviewed about how they interacted with one another and about who else were powerful members of the community.

Dahl used an entirely different method, selecting several important community decisions (e.g., urban renewal, education) on which official decisions had recently been made, and examining the history of public negotiations leading to those decisions.

"Pluralist" theorists, such as Dahl (1961) and Polsby (1980), fault the "reputational" method for guaranteeing its own findings. True, they concede, members of a community find the question "who has power around here" intelligible, and can even come to a consensus about the answer. But pluralists argue that this is just rumor or hearsay, and has no necessary bearing on the actual functioning of power. They prefer the scientifically ascetic method of restricting their conclusions to those that may be drawn from the public record rather than focusing on unverifiable myths about pulling the strings "behind the scenes." When this is done, investigators quite reliably see competition among groups, each of which has sufficient resources to keep the others from having their way all the time, and all of whom are "kept honest" by the underlying fear of an outraged mass electorate pulling the plug on them.

Adherents of the reputational method retort that the pluralists, too, guarantee their findings by choice of method. By restricting their attention to publicly debated governmental decisions, it is held, pluralists see only those issues on which the clique holding real power is either split or indifferent. Other issues, including most of the important ones, are "settled out of court" without either public display or public participation. The "potential" power of the mass electorate, they insist, is even more of a mythical entity than the power of economic notables operating through their publicly visible representatives, for patently the electorate lacks information and other resources (most people, after all, do not vote), whereas the group in power just as obviously has the ability to exercise pressure if and when it chooses to do so.

The debate that continued for the next decade or so was at times quite ill-tempered, for each side saw the other as fanatically preoccupied with an epiphenomenon falsely labeled as power. The issue of reliability, then, became over time one of validity. The real disagreement between the two traditions was about the definition of power. To the pluralists, power is the likelihood of prevailing over another who is actively seeking a contradictory goal. To partisans of the reputational method, power is the likelihood of getting one's way. When the community behaves by default (rather than as a consequence of a public decision) in such a way as to benefit some person or group, these latter see power in action; the former do not. To those who study power by reputation, the status quo and prevailing definitions of the appropriate topics for political debate are power resources in the hands of those who benefit from them. To those who study political debate, power is only one way of obtaining benefit from the community, and the individual or members of a group who get goodies simply because they have always gotten them is not employing power.

Both the reliability issue and the subsequent validity issue proved highly productive, and after another decade or so the sharpness of the debate has tempered.[22] The question of reliability led to studies like Freeman's (1968), in which a reputation for power was seen to coincide with multiple organizational connections and participation in a wide variety of public decisions, and Clark's (1971) comparative studies of the consequences of power. The validity issue has profoundly clarified conceptual issues about power, and led to highly sophisticated models (Emerson, 1962; March, 1966; Coleman, 1973).

DAUGHTERS AND FATHERS

Recently, Freeman (1983) has confirmed the relevance of diachronic reliability to study and restudy comparisons in qualitative research. Freeman impeaches Mead's (1928) early ethnographic conclusions, most notably that anger, violence, and competition are neutralized in Samoan culture.[23] Freeman and Mead also differ substantially in their respective evaluations of adolescent sexual behavior.

By Mead's report, virginity at marriage is nominally important in Samoan society, but teenagers systematically engage in considerable expert and playful sex. According to Freeman, this misrepresents the facts. The cult of virginity, he argues, is taken very seriously by traditional and contemporary Samoans. Female virgins are highly valued, eagerly sought after, and zealously protected by male kin.

The discrepancy between the observations of Mead and Freeman compel a discussion of reliability. Indeed, Freeman effectively finesses the issue of diachronic reliability, presenting historical and survey evidence to indicate that the Samoa he studied had not been radically transfigured during the decades after Mead's visit. Freeman, then, sees this as an issue of synchronic reliability. Naturally, he regards his own conclusions as internally reliable and those of Mead as counterfeit.

There is an alternative to choosing between Mead and Freeman. The possibility of accepting both sets of findings, however, requires a theory of how Mead and Freeman obtained the different results that they did. Mead talked with female adolescents at a time she herself was a young woman. Freeman conducted much of his study of Samoa with male parents at a time he himself was a high-ranking adult. Mead's and Freeman's conclusions are together based on the interplay of the field researcher and the studied culture, but this case study may boil down to different investigators observing different parts of the same Samoan scene.

Indeed, the sexual behavior of adolescents is a touchy subject and Samoans are inclined to be insulted by the suggestion that Samoan teenagers are promiscuous. (This reminds one of Malinowski's famous passage about a Martian anthropologist asking a British aristocrat whether adulterous hanky-panky goes on in the Commonwealth.) It is possible that Samoan culture is not so different from contemporary American culture on the score of adolescent sex. By analogy, an American daughter might well tell (to a young and female adult ethnographer) some pretty interesting stories based on considerable sophistication; at the same time, an American male parent might assert (to an adult male ethnographer) that his daughters are virgin. By the same token, the father's description of his work life as a "rat race" might seem inconsistent with the daughter's characterization of her Daddy and his friends as "nice men."

The point here is that Freeman's findings do not necessarily refute Mead's, or vice-versa. Mead and Freeman were on to different aspects of a very large and complex subject. The partial understandings they achieved are different for good reason, and we are better off with both sets of findings than only one.

EXTRAS

One of the things that Rasmussen (Douglas, 1976) wanted to know about the local massage parlors was whether they were sex-for-money shops. To investigate, Rasmussen started hanging out in one near his home, talking, drinking, and joking with the employees. Evidently, he achieved a very high level of friendly rapport. In answer to his casual questions about sex with customers, he was consistently told by his informants that they gave no "extras." They conceded that some masseuses at some parlors might be out-and-out prostitutes, but pointed out a variety of reasons why they preferred to sell the fantasy instead of the reality.

Douglas, supervising the research, argues in favor of two rules of thumb for investigative research in general: (a) "Where there's smoke, there's fire," (and, "Where there's some fire, there's bound to be more fire"), and (b) "There's always far more immoral or shady stuff going on than meets the eye." He recommended greater skepticism to Rasmussen (Douglas, 1976). Accordingly,

Rasmussen sought other sources of information, such as his barber, who frequented the parlors. Reports from the other sources agreed completely with what the masseuses told him. Professor Douglas, nonetheless, continued to insist on the principle that people in general "have good reason to hide from others what they are doing and even to lie to them," so Rasmussen continued to hang around. Finally, one of his informants, somehow assuming that Rasmussen already knew the whole truth, made reference to some of the illegal sexual activities she was involved in on the job. Confronted with certain details, Rasmussen's prime informants (and close friends) admitted that what they had told him earlier was not quite complete. After a few iterations of the "phased-assertion" technique of seeming already to know, Rasmussen concluded that sex for money, if not entirely universal, was centrally endemic to the industry.

Any war story may be used to illustrate any of several points. Douglas tells the one above to illustrate that friendly rapport by itself is not enough. For that matter, Rasmussen would perhaps have had far less trouble getting at the truth if his informants had personally liked him less. Rasmussen's story has much in common with feeding coca to the animals (Chapter 2). In both cases, the investigator's initial questions were familiar, and characteristic of a certain social role familiar to the informants (tourists, in the Peruvian case; boyfriends, in Rasmussen's). Therefore, they elicited a practiced "party line" specifically organized for delivery to those in the role signified by the question.

Rasmussen's validity problem was trivial. His informants were lying to him, and he knew it (or at least Professor Douglas knew it). The Peruvian waiters who told the authors about coca were doing something considerably more subtle. Taking the facts for granted, they delivered to the researchers the culturally approved interpretation. In the Peruvian case, the problem of reliability was equally trivial. The excessive and quixotic reliability of the responses the authors received early on was so blatant as to tip them off that they were hearing a number of readings of the same script. Rasmussen's early information was synchronically, rather than quixotically reliable. He talked at length with different masseuses, as well as people in client and owner roles. They all told him different things, which agreed only on the point at issue: that sex was not for sale in the parlor. Nothing about his early data indicated that he was not receiving the whole truth. He finally stumbled on it for two reasons. First, like Malinowski, he "spent enough time in the field." Although there are probably some things about the parlor that he understood better during his first five minutes than after he had more nearly gone native, the carefully organized deceptive front simply developed no cracks for many, many hours. Second, Douglas was willing to look a fool for the sake of science.

The Reporting of "Raw" Data

The familiar parable of the blind men and the elephant illustrates the problem of reliability. According to that story, several blind men encountered an elephant, investigated its various parts, and quarreled over their mutually irreconcilable reports.

The thesis/punch line, or *chiste*, of the parable is not to poke fun at the visually impaired but to dramatize the imperfection of the various epistemic positions that can be taken with regard to such stories. A vulgar positivist might be imagined to take some sort of statistical average of the data ("compensating for error in measurement"), and conclude that the elephant is a formless blob covered with elephant skin.[24] The original interpretation seems to have been what Hirsch (1976) calls "intuitionist." The problem with the intuitionist interpretation (that the elephant cannot be known by observation) is that unless certain priests' claims to vision are validated by instituted authority, it provides no means to resolve differing interpretations.

Hirsch also rejects a third position, "perspectivism," in its pure phenomenological form. In that form, perspectivism treats all interpretations (perspectives) as equally valid, and explicitly denies the possibility of mediating among them. As Hirsch suggests, there is no such thing as "raw data" in the purest sense. Human beings do not simply perceive, then interpret, but rather go through a process called cognition. The normal adult human is not ordinarily fooled by his or her visual perspective into thinking people walking toward him or her are growing taller, or that a disc seen from an angle is elliptical. Prior to interpreting cognitive experience, people match visual and other input with stored percepts in particular ways. This is to say they actually require a theory (e.g., of stimulus constancy) in order to be able to see an object as approaching rather than growing. (For a discussion of current psychological views of this process, see Anderson, 1980.)

Data, then, can only be reported in terms of some explicit or implicit theory. That the theories people use to perceive are not altogether culture-free is shown by a variety of studies (see Segall et al., 1966). These studies show also that some theories are better for perceiving some things, whereas other theories work better for perceiving others. With a theory that the elephant is so large and complex that no single observation can encompass it, the various blind men's reports can be integrated without the necessity of special occult vision. With no interpretive theory, we may forget that there is an elephant out there and simply marvel that the blind men can report anything at all.[25] For present purposes, however, it is more important that if the blind men themselves (the field researchers) have an initial notion that each feels only a part of some huge object, their reports will not even be apparently contradictory. As Maquet (1964) has observed, "A perspectivistic knowledge is not as such nonobjective; it is partial. . . . Nonobjectivity creeps in when the partial aspect is considered as the global one."

Reliability, then—like validity—is meaningful only by reference to some theory. The implicit theory that requires all observations to be identical is rarely appropriate. In the natural sciences, this quixotic reliability is only expected in artificial experimental situations. Observational sciences generally rely on the contrast between things that change (as planets) and those that stay relatively the same (as "fixed" stars).

Even within psychometrics, where the issue of reliability was first made explicit, the demand for quixotic reliability creates irresolvable theoretical paradoxes. Both intelligence and personality tests were originally designed as therapeutic tools; to measure (or bring about) change in a variable designed to reflect unchanging dispositions is futile by definition.

FIELDNOTES AS A RELIABILITY CHECK

To place an observation in perspective in a theoretical context, the analyst wishes to know as much as possible about the cognitive idiosyncracies of the observer—which is to say about his or her theories. These theories include not only academic commitments but also values, behavioral style, and experience— features that are often classified as part of "personality." In everyday life, in historiography, in legal proceedings, and in journalistic reportage, much is made of the nature of the source. Too often, in blind imitation of the reporting style of natural science, a pretense is made by social scientists of being "neutral observers." Of course, this constitutes the arrogant claim to be a sighted person in a world of blind men, but worse, it fails to reflect the feature of natural-science reporting it is designed to emulate. Laboratory experiments are intended to display the effects of interaction among a very small number of variables, and all the "relevant" variables are reported.[26] The field observations of qualitative research intrinsically involve the observer, whereas the observations made in a chemistry lab do so minimally if at all.

The theory we all share about chemical observations is that the same observation will be made whether or not the observer is suffering from insect bites or malnutrition; extending that assumption to the ethnographic observer of a tropical village is doubtful. When the observation is presented stripped of information about how it was collected, the reader is unable to place any meaningful interpretation on it because the status of relevant variables is unspecified. The chemist who reports that he or she obtained an explosion has little trouble knowing that what reagents he or she used is relevant; the participant observer who begins without a clearly specified list of relevant variables may in a misguided attempt at scientific modesty and "objectivity" refuse to report equally relevant context. To do so is as arrogant as the chemist refusing to report his or her ingredients.

Qualitative research has developed a number of conventions that aggravate the problem. Typically, the same individual collects the data and presents an analysis of it (and, unfortunately, is not always aware of which he or she is doing at a particular point). Finished ethnographies are professionally circulated; once in a while they are supplemented by discussions of field methods (because competing methods are more often used in the field, qualitative researchers from the discipline of sociology have traditionally been rather better at this than those from anthropology); rarely has any researcher (or student) actually seen another's field notes. Fieldworkers studying weak or oppressed groups are professionally bound to take the role of protector of those groups: This not only leads to an inclination to "launder" reports (Douglas, 1976), but discourages "poaching" on a colleague's "territory."

Working ethnographers know they can report only what happened to them in the field, not what life there was like before they arrived. Yet to raise questions about the reliability of another's observations is taboo, as though it were an accusation of incompetence, bias, or dishonesty.

THE NATURE OF FIELDNOTES

The contemporary search for reliability in qualitative observation revolves around detailing the relevant context of observation. W. F. Whyte (1955) discussed in revealing detail his experiences and the way he arrived at the methods he used. Others have issued personal statements about their experiences in the field (Bowen, 1954; Dumont, 1978; Levi-Strauss, 1961; Van Maanen, 1982, and many others), which serve not only to orient the reader both to the interpersonal and cognitive style of the researcher but also to his or her theoretical and methodological commitments. Toward the end of distinguished careers, auto-biographical essays are frequently published (Powdermaker, 1966; Mead, 1972; Anderson, 1980). None of these confessions, however, seems to help us understand the context of observation sufficiently to shed new light on the observations actually made. They are ordinarily relegated to separate appendices or (worse) to separate volumes. Divorced once more from the data and from the situation in which it was collected, these self-interpretations of the investigator tend to suffer from the same uncritical cognition and leaps of interpretive logic as do the interpretations of the target of study by the same researchers. This will inevitably be the case, even for those who can heroically resist the temptation to launder their own autobiographies.

Frake (1964) has pointed out that whereas the ethnographic record of qualitative researchers has traditionally consisted of lists of questions and answers, "the tradition in modern anthro-pology . . . is not to make such a record public but to publish an essay about it." The ethnographer, according to Black and Metzger (1965), "needs to know what question people are answering in their every act. He needs to know which questions are being taken for granted because they are what 'everybody knows' without thinking."

From Mead to Whiting et al. (1966), efforts have been made to "standardize" questions and the recording of observations. These efforts are designed to introduce into qualitative observation some of the reliability characteristic of laboratory and survey methods. Unfortunately, as Labov and Fanshel (1977) comment about psychotherapeutic interviews, reports of such standardized interviews and observations sometimes provide so little of the broader ethnographic context that the relevance of their reliable findings to their conclusions is suspect. Excessive standardization deliberately abandons the attempt to discover things more accessible to some observers than to others.

A casual example of Mead's (1965) technique displays the limits of standardization. In explaining to high school students the nature of fieldwork, she asked her colleagues similar questions:

"Professor Arensberg, you're a social anthropologist, aren't you?"

"Yes."

. . .

"Dr. Bunzel, you are Adjunct Professor of Anthropology at Columbia, is that right?"

"That's right."

. . .

"Professor Solecki, you're an archaeologist, aren't you?"

"Yes."

The "standardization" of questions here goes part way toward the reinvention of the social survey, a retrogressive move that seeks quixotic reliability at the expense of validity. Mead, however, was too good a fieldworker to be able to ask identical questions of everyone. Professor Arensberg is not addressed as "Dr. Bunzel," or accused of being an archaeologist. Like all competent fieldworkers, Mead used what she already knew about the target culture to phrase her questions. (Whether any of her high school audience could have chanced upon the correct questions is a different issue.) The reader, however, can place an interpretation on the otherwise uninformative answers ("Yes," and "That's right.") if and only if the reader knows the question.

CONVENTIONALIZED FIELDNOTES

One reason fieldnotes are rarely published or distributed is that they tend to be entirely unintelligible to anyone who does not take for granted the same things as did the fieldworker at the time the notes were recorded. Indeed, qualitative researchers commonly find their own earlier notes ambiguous or incomprehensible, because they have forgotten what it was that they knew or felt when the notes were taken. Recording the questions that were asked contributes a great deal to the meaningfulness of notes. (As Black and Metzger point out, the ultimate aid in understanding the answers would be a record not of what the fieldworker thought she was asking, but of what the informant heard. Unfortunately, this is rarely possible.)

For many purposes (particularly for studying relatively familiar groups), recording questions, and to some degree standardizing them, is not only a necessary step, but a sufficient one. For other purposes, emulation of laboratory protocols, closed-end interview schedules, or linguistic eliciting techniques is not sufficient. (Berreman lists these other purposes as "understanding how people relate to one another and to their environment, what is the nature of their social interaction, and how it relates to their values, emotions, attitudes, and self-conceptions; their hopes and fears.") For those purposes, "extensive, explicit, and perceptive field notes, self-analytical reporting of research procedures and research contexts, documentation of sources, documentation of the bases for inferences, and documentation of the ethnographer's theories of society and his biases" (Berreman, 1966) are important.

Spradley (1979) recommends four separate "kinds of field notes": the condensed (verbatim) account, an expanded account recorded as soon as possible after each field session, a "field work journal" that contains "experiences, ideas, fears, mistakes, confusions, breakthroughs, and problems that arise during field work," and a provisional running record of analysis and interpretation. Both paradigms demand that certain minimal requirements be met. Entries must be legible and chronologically identified. They must clearly differentiate among various kinds of entry, and must record native-language utterances as nearly verbatim as possible. (This last requirement entails certain necessary syntactic and diacritical deviations from prose writing.)

The emerging conventionalization of field-note format performs a variety of services beyond making reliability possible. It encourages the incorporation of socially undesirable but revealing content (selfish thoughts, obscene or racist remarks, wild speculations, theoretically unpalatable interpretations, and other "irresponsible" material of the sort that Malinowski relegated to his *Diary*). That the researcher might be unwilling to display such idiosyncratic passing thoughts to his or her informants, to professional adversaries, or to his or her close friends should not, as it has tended to in the past, inhibit their recording. Freed from the necessity to be "responsible" for the interpretive content of the notes, the researcher is also at liberty to record obvious errors. As suggested in the first chapter of this essay, the role played by stupid mistakes in the history of science is impressive; Agar (1983) advocates an active search by qualitative researchers for "anti-coherence." These mistakes are of particular importance in the study of groups initially unfamiliar to the researcher. As Mead (1973) remarks, "when the field worker arrives in his field, work begins immediately; there are first impressions that will not be repeated and so must be recorded." The more the fieldworker "goes native" by understanding and identifying with the target group, the less accessible such "naive" impressions become, and the researcher, if he or she has failed to record them, may lose access to his or her own first impressions and responses.

The ostensible purpose of fieldnote conventionalization, facilitating exchange of notes among colleagues, seems to be enhanced rather than inhibited by the decreased laundering that occurs. Not only is it always possible to withhold or censor field notes, but when the sharing of notes is reciprocal a highly cooperative, rather than adversarial, relationship among colleagues develops. Many of those currently experimenting with the exchange of field notes of the informal and uncensored variety find that the prospect of sharing such confessional notes with

Diacritical	Convention	Use
" "	double quotation marks	contain verbatim quotes
' '	single quotation marks	contain paraphrases
( )	parentheses	encloses contextual data and/or fieldworker's interpretation
< >	angle brackets	denotes elements of emic lexicon
_____	solid line	partitions time
/	slash	denotes emic contrast

Figure 5.1 Basic Fieldnote Conventions

supportive colleagues actually encourages the verbalization of shameful (but often analytically useful) notions.

A GUIDE TO FIELDNOTE STYLE

Fieldnotes, however unique the fieldworker, must conform to several minimal requirements. First, field entries must be legible and chronologically ordered. Second, entries must differentiate among categories of data (e.g., what people literally say, the unobtrusively measured "context" of social interactions, what the ethnographer preliminarily hypothesizes about the situation).

The general strategy for the recording of culturally meaningful utterances (i.e., the things that people say) is to build from a foundation of modern orthography, and to depart from general editorial style as necessary to ensure faithfulness to the original comment. For example, capital letters and periods may be used when complete sentences are recorded. Similarly, quotation marks, including those for quotes within quotes, may also be employed. However, fieldnote punctuation should definitely facilitate the recording of incomplete thoughts.

Figure 5.1 presents a basic inventory of diacritical conventions for taking ethnographic fieldnotes.

To illustrate the use of these conventions, Figure 5.2 displays a portion of fieldnotes recorded by the authors in beginning stages

Sunday 24 June 1984 4:27 p.m.

WINDSURFING CLUB
inside:
walk in to "Surfin' USA"

"Daddy, you have to go by the hot tub to get to the deck!"
   (not to mention equipment and fashion section, sauna, locker rooms, weight room, deli, tanning stations. . . .)

---

video repeats Columbia Gorge windsurfing

---

outside:
now there are three decks (seasonal fill-ins between slips).
   south (newest) deck: instruction. two training units on deck
      middle deck: ". . . now it's the restaurant. The new deck is for instruction . . .
      and the old deck is for members (to sunbathe)."
   north deck: sunning on blue outdoor carpet (?) but no lounge chairs.

---

9 people	2 taking lessons; 2 sunning	not crowded
6 women	3 tables	
3 men	2 employees (?)	

<short boom / ('regular boom')>

'What does this place resemble to you?'
"Well, you know, I was raised in Europe . . . Lake Geneva. . . ."
   (he insists he approves of the "chaos" of Seattle's urban waterfront)

Beginners are on strings

<duck tack/helicopter tack>
<duck jibe>

1984 HiFly 300
   $600

---

by surfing standards, even the state-of-the-art [production boards]
   (e.g., HiFly 320) are heavy

ATTENTION SEATTLE HARBOR PATROL REQUIRES ALL WINDSURFERS TO
WEAR A HARNESS OR PERSONAL FLOTATION DEVICES
   (posted: "it just happened, it's the law" . . . even for instructors . . .')

can't tell employees from the members/guests. employees may be younger.

harbor police cruise slowly 20' from the dock between 6 windsurfers. None of whom
have flotation anything. no action.

Figure 5.2   Fieldnotes re: Lake Union Leisure

of the study of water leisure. The fieldnotes refer to the cultural scene at an elite club in Seattle.

6. ETHNOGRAPHIC DECISION MAKING: THE FOUR PHASES OF QUALITATIVE RESEARCH

Writing a communicable account of a complex event in a social situation requires not only a high degree of literacy but at least some comprehension of the social science purposes for which the record may have its uses. It is a task in which the beginner and professional social scientist, if they were to compare notes, might find that they have more in common than either would suppose. The experienced observer encounters phenomena and deals with a social rhetoric that he or she aims to record in its natural freshness—not as something to be assimilated immediately to a theoretical system that usefully compares analogues but that, if imposed upon the situation of observation, may rob it of the opportunity to reveal something new. The task is not greatly different for the beginner. Despite any social science theoretical system to which he or she has been exposed, the novice has not had so many direct experiences with textbook analogues that they threaten to intervene between his or her recording and his or her observation or between his or her perception and the event. In their place, the novice has the handicaps of at least his or her cultural training to overcome if the novice is to learn to do fieldwork for a social science.

> For expert or student, therefore, the whole point of devoting time to recording is not merely to make sure he will have materials down in black and white upon which to base his final report, but also to insure that he has the opportunity, while in the field or fresh from it, to relate insightful experience to theoretical analysis, percept to concept, back and forth, in a kind of weaving of the fabric of knowledge [Junker, 1960: 13].

Qualitative research, like other science, is a four-phase affair. Accordingly, the full qualitative effort depends upon the ordered sequence of invention, discovery, interpretation, and explanation.[27] Importantly, the bundles of research activities performed in each of these phases, or modes, differ qualitatively from one another. So, too, are the research products generated in each phase. *Invention* denotes a phase of preparation, or research design; this phase produces a plan of action. *Discovery* denotes a phase of observation and measurement, or data collection; this phase produces information. *Interpretation* denotes a phase of evaluation, or analysis; this phase produces understanding. *Explanation* denotes a phase of communication, or packaging; this phase produces a message.

The rules of qualitative research are simple. First, all of the four phases must figure in the research. In no sense are the phases substitutes for one another. Second, the phases must be completed in the proper sequence. Critically, and whatever the corrections made in the course of research, the phase products depend upon one another in only one way.

The four phases of qualitative research find expression in activities and products that themselves can be catalogued at different levels of abstraction and according to different time frames. Microscopically, for example, we can imagine how the four phases might shape the process by which we search for paradigmatically influential materials in an unfamiliar literature, or manage to put a thought to paper in a report. At the macroscopic extreme, we can imagine the role of the four phases in the coordination of a series of interdependent research projects, or the unfolding of a professional career. In what follows, the four phases are shown to partition the period of time ethnographic researchers spend in the field.

Fieldwork

Nothing is easier than to do anthropological work of a certain sort, but to get to the bottom of native customs and modes of thought, and to record the results of inquiry in such a manner that they carry conviction, is work which can only be carried out properly by careful attention to method [Royal Anthropological Institute, 1929: 29].

Direct observation supplemented by immediate interrogation is the ideal course; it is most satisfactory to begin an investigation into any particular subject by way of direct observation of some event, and follow it up by questions as to details, variations, similar events, etc. This may not always be possible [Royal Anthropological Institute, 1951: 27].

Of all the activities of qualitative researchers, fieldwork is most responsible for the mystique and popular image of ethnography. Interaction with people on their own turf and in their own language, and the systematic recording of it all are the bare essentials of fieldwork. Fieldwork has two strong connotations. By the first extreme coding, fieldwork is an extraordinarily expressive opportunity to learn everything about a new culture from scratch. With this orientation, ethnographers experience the wonder of the world in the role of the child. By the second extreme coding, fieldwork is an exceedingly instrumental opportunity to gather specific facts. With this orientation, ethnographers experience the tediousness of science in the role of the "lab assistant." But these codings have little programmatic utility. To define fieldwork so broadly that it equates with life itself provides no guidelines for decisions. To define fieldwork narrowly is to deny that decisions are needed at all. A major procedural concern for fieldworkers, then, is knowing how to determine if one is discovering or interpreting or inventing or explaining. Plainly, ethnographers operate in all of these modes while in the field.

For qualitative researchers, fieldwork is heavily loaded with symbolism and import. It is with fieldwork that the substance of ethnographic data is generated. The fact that fieldwork is universally understood by professionals to separate a "Before Data" period from an "After Data" period is essential to its role as a rite of passage. With the accumulation of data, the ethnographer moves from the state of research preparation to the state of research analysis.

The four phases of qualitative research map easily to the fieldwork period. The phases directly correspond to problem solving associated with "finding," "working," "reading," and "leaving" the field.

INVENTION: "GETTING IN" AND "GETTING ALONG"

If there is one binding common experience to be found across more than one hundred years of ethnographic inquiry, it encompasses the moments of finding the field. Contemplation of what it means to confront an exotic culture is a time-honored meditation that not only figures prominently in the recruitment of students to the study of human patterns but also inspires and consolidates the culture of field researchers. The great empathy ethnographers demonstrate for one another when the war stories of "getting in" and "getting along" are recounted underscores a shared awareness of the personal tribulations, symptomatic vulnerability, and odd courage of the field researcher species.

Unless the planned research is basically surreptitious in nature, at no time are ethnographers so aware of their innocence as at the time of first contact. There are, no doubt, many examples of fieldworkers who never attained a status accorded by people studied of anyone more complicated than a hopeless fool or a dull stranger. Nonetheless, fieldworkers in their own eyes grow wise through fieldwork.

Fieldwork and intellectual progress are made most evident by the staggering qualitative difference between what the ethnographer knew at the outset of field research and what he or she came to know later. In academia, the assertion by an ethnographer that he or she qualifies as a Field Sage is not always followed quickly by community congratulations. However, when one claims to have been a Field Fool, collegial annointment is considerably less problematic. The ranks of Sage and Fool depend on one another in the strategic sense that some Sages are understood to be ex-Fools. If the fieldworker can provide data to the academic community suggesting he or she was once a Fool, the fieldworker improves his or her chances of making Sage.

For these reasons, the scenario of the noble fieldworker first arriving on the scene and handily demonstrating ignorance to local culture is universally acted out by ethnographers. The offshoot of this is that all ethnographers (for their own protection and aspiration) have a favorite and well-rehearsed "getting-in" war story.

Generally speaking, the first several waves of ethnographers who insisted, as a matter of professional birthright, on the opportunity to conduct fieldwork reported little difficulty in physically locating societies to study. Whether the cultures of concern were organized by Native Americans in the Pacific Northwest, European immigrants in greater Chicago, island peoples in Oceania, or colonized British subjects elsewhere, eager fieldworkers established expectations that the major problems of locating a tribe would be logistical (i.e., not methodological or theoretical). The original algorithm for Finding the Field under early circumstances was something on the order of

(1) pick a continent, or set of islands, or a suburb;
(2) find someone connected in some way (e.g., social service, ecclesiastic, commercial) to both the Western culture of orientation and the people to be studied;
(3) accept a ride (or at least directions) in the field.

Roughly speaking, Finding the Field starts when the ethnographer leaves his hometown and ends just before the ethnographer arranges the first systematic collection of data. Three aspects of this "Ethnography at the periphery" are defined by the securing of first directions, first views, and first conclusions.

Copping Directions. Copping Directions is the first aspect of Finding the Field. It pertains to the moments of networking across social systems to the express end of arriving at the culture to be studied. It is the popular image of field research that ethnographers, whether aided by supreme luck, guile, or money, gravitate effortlessly to the hubs of culture, action, and influence. Somehow, the imperative "Take me to your leader" is thought to engender quick results, to be intrinsically meaningful, and to be an appeal worthy of serious attention by anyone in the world.

This romantic script of how ethnographers establish contact with societies they study ignores the role of intermediaries who arrange the Grand Entrance of the heroic field researcher. Intermediaries (e.g., missionaries, merchants, administrators) operate at the fringes and borders of cultures and are among the first in any society to denounce, proselytize, and straddle cultural systems. Often stigmatized as eccentric, deviant, and mission-oriented, the intermediaries are the prototypical marginal citizens. They are innovative in their interaction with air-dropped field researchers for the basic motives of curiosity, profit, and, in some cases, altruism.

Copping a Look. Copping a Look is the second aspect of Finding the Field. It concerns the moments of first viewing a culture. As simple as this experience sounds, it is a nagging paradox of human studies that social scenes and cultural settings (to scramble Spradley and Lofland terminologies) evaporate as the well-intentioned ethnographer comes up close.

It is a naive notion that sociological concepts such as culture, society, community, and tribe cleanly map onto the legally calculated physical territories of the world. Ironically, anthropologists have substantiated this view of a Disney-partitioned cultural universe with their remarkable record of locating "lost" peoples. The ethnographic literature seems replete with expedition sagas detailing the formidable obstructions presented by jungle, mountain, and other nefarious no-man's-lands. Victorious over the elements, and first viewing the culture of study, the level-headed ethnographer is seen in the classic view to be unswayed by the seductions of sentiment and to be true to the principles of detached observation. Of course, history has shown this has not universally been the case.

Copping a Taste. Copping a Taste is the third aspect of Finding the Field. This very American terminology for the moments of first cultural readings suggestively hints at the elements of surprise, invasion, strategy, pleasure, and excitement that characterize the motivation and response of both parties in the coming together of native and ethnographer. The period of Copping a Taste consists of the early episodes of unobtrusive (or at least "free-form") assessment of host and guest cultures. It is a time for preconceptions to be shattered, unanticipated constraints to emerge, and bases for bias to be identified.

DISCOVERY: "GETTING DATA"

The discovery phase of fieldwork is the ethnographic process of collecting data. Working the Field roughly begins when the field researcher instrumentally concerns him- or herself with identifying a specific time and place to conduct an observation or inquiry. The phase ends when the ethnographer has obtained an appropriate quantity and quality of data over the course of multiple exposures to, and interactions with, the people under study.

Amassing of data in the field is a ritualistic test of great significance within the culture of qualitative social science—ethnographic data in hand is worth twenty times that amount in the bush. Once the fieldworker has command over the data, he or she has jumped the midpoint hurdle in the research process. The fieldworker has faced the unknown native in his or her own language and on his or her own turf, and has secured data that has meaning for him or her.

Working the Field pertains to the settling down of the ethnographer to the actual business of recording information. Three aspects of Working the Field are defined by the discovery of opportunities, data, and closure.

Scoring a Chance. Field research conducted without attention to the native perception and local cultural context of ethnography is a contradiction in terms. Presumably, such abuses are indicated in the varied ways ethnographers pursue and maintain kinds of rapport. The first aspect of Working the Field concerns preparations and the securing of an opening for data collection. These logistics and exercises in rapport are termed Scoring a Chance. Preparation alludes to topics that include the strategic presentation of the ethnographer's persona, the development of research instruments, the location of key and other informants, and the coordination of a research situation (i.e., a task environment). Success in this endeavor is no mean feat of cultural choreography.

Scoring the Facts. Scoring the Facts denotes the very essence of Working the Field—the hands-on real work of gathering ethnographic data. At first impressionistic glance, it would seem that the Scoring of Facts can be approached and conducted in a straightforward manner. To this, two comments are in order.

First, any possibility of a smoothly running fact collecting field operation is critically dependent on a plan of research action. It is unscientific as well as maddening to initiate data collection without a language (paradigm) that precisely contrasts data and noise. The ethnographer who gathers without knowing what he or she wants (at the logical level) will find no happiness in the process.

Second, the Scoring of Facts in the field research application is a multifaceted affair. Clearly, the focal activity must be the systematic (i.e., research design specified) amassing of information. But, even as this goes on, the field research has the opportunity to consider tangential issues of any order. That is, the ethnographer is, at one and the same time, Scoring the Facts and discovering new kinds of facts (those *not* being collected).

Scoring the Facts primarily involves the gathering of data, but extends to considerable hypothesizing from that activity. Though perhaps too glib, it is almost fair to say that qualitative research is defined by the location of hypothesis-testing activity in the discovery, rather than the interpretation, phase. Scoring the Facts begins with the formal effort to gather information, inquiries, on-the-scene modification of procedure, and terminates with data in hand.

Scoring an Ending. The third aspect of Working the Field has to do with the circumstances by which the process of Scoring the Facts is terminated. Scoring an Ending pertains to the final moments of individual interviews, observation sessions, and the like. Importantly, Scoring an Ending is not always desired by the ethnographer. Endings of data gathering can be caused by acts of God, inadvertent insult, depletion of funds, and social fatigue, as well as by attainment of research objectives. The reality of field research is that, once engaged, the two parties of the data-collecting encounter cannot be expected to separate gratefully with equivalent satisfaction about the exchange.

More often than not, field researchers have attended less to the winding down of fieldwork than they would care to admit. Certainly, ethnographers exhibit concern when they are victims of breakdowns in Scoring the Facts (for example, scoring a brush-off; scoring a lie; scoring wrong data). But there are also lessons in understanding to externalities of "successful" data recovery efforts.

INTERPRETATION: "GETTING IT STRAIGHT"

Reading the Field has its locus in interpretive moments following the discovery of ethnographic data. It is in this subphase that the field researcher begins to ponder the validity, reliability, and overall meaning of materials. It is also a time of readjusting rapport, recalibrating tools, and redesigning field strategems. Reading the Field begins as the field researcher accumulates ethnographic evidence, continues through the (sometimes radical) bargaining of research objectives, and winds down as the field researcher is wedded to a complete data set.

A distinguishing and favorite feature of the ethnographic process commonly cited by practitioners is that the ethnographer finds him- or herself in a position to chronicle cultural performances primarily as a consequence of remaining on the scene long enough to witness the full cycles of cultural routines, as well as long enough to dispel native anxieties concerning the fate of collected information. What this means is that the field researcher is exposed to generically similar human situations, roles, behaviors, beliefs, and so on from a variety of vantage points. This occurs with the interpretative assistance of informants and local observers of the scenes. When things go smoothly, the ethnographer watches his or her confusion turn to tentative hypothesis. He or she probably also notices that his or her hunches require reformulation, and his or her pet theories may crumble apart. Such is the scientific endeavor.

The field researcher engaged in Reading the Field is struggling to understand how the data he or she has amassed qualify as information (rather than noise), and how they are amenable to analysis. When the process proceeds smoothly, there is a gradual verification of a hypothesized relation between the research problem, tools, and data. The ethnographer becomes alert to the reaction he or she has prompted, keen to the fact that ethnography is not a report on a people but a report on the encounter between the researcher and the tribe. When things do not go smoothly—when there is a breakdown—the ethnographer must adjust the problem, the tools, or his or her reading of the data.

The work of Reading the Field correctly is a process part of the test tradition of science. There is always the chance that the blunders, mistakes, and errors that constitute "getting it wrong" and that are so integral to "getting it right" may become the anomalies that herald Discovery.

We isolate two aspects of Reading the Field, both of which incorporate the themes of reappraisal, iteration, and convergence. These concern questioning the meaning and strength of the facts.

Checking the Validity. The first aspect of Reading the Field is labeled, "Checking the Validity." This is primarily an evaluation of Working the Field. As such, it calls for a consideration of the components of the research situation (place, time, informant) and the research problem and tools. At issue is the validity of observations (i.e., whether or not the researcher is calling what is measured by the right name).

Checking the Reliability. The second aspect of Reading the Field involves checking the strength of the data. This is purely and simply the exercise of investigating the reliability of qualitative research. The issue is one of whether or not (or under what conditions) the ethnographer would expect to obtain the same funding if he or she tried again in the same way.

EXPLANATION: "GETTING OUT" AND "GETTING EVEN"

The explanation phase of fieldwork concerns the ethnographic process of Leaving the Field. This process begins with the realization by the ethnographer that an adequate qualitative data base has been secured, and ends when the fieldworker returns home.

The field exit is much more than a matter of packing and perfunctory good-byes. It is a phase of research in which foreign and native parties to the ethnographic contract settle accounts (as well as establish groundrules for future communication and interaction). Thus the professional ethic requires attention to the rights and obligations of "getting even" in the course of "getting out."

Leaving the Field is a phase based on closure and departure. Three aspects of Leaving the Field are defined by separations from relationships, costs and benefits, and the field.

Splitting-Up. The first aspect of Leaving the Field centers around the severing of professional working relationships. It is at this time that the qualitative researcher disassociates him- or herself from field assistants, informants, bureaucracies, and the suppliers of incidental materials.

Splitting the Take. The second aspect of Leaving the Field concerns the negotiations between the fieldworker and the studied population of how the costs and benefits of the research shall be allocated. At this time, the fieldworker must resolve how he or she is to reimburse the studied culture in exchange for the research opportunity, and what will be the consequence for individuals and the community when the new local role, field-worker, is suddenly vacant.

Splitting-the-Scene. The third aspect of Leaving the Field involves the physical distancing of the qualitative researcher from the research site. This process entails the last readings, sightings, and directions the ethnographer obtains through fieldwork.

Using This Book

This volume began with the general observation that qualitative researchers find difficulty in defining their methods. In particular, those qualitative researchers who have preferred not to equate techniques of participant observation, ethnomethodology, frame analysis, and the like strictly with "artistic," "poetic," and "humanistic" processes have fared poorly in justifying their professional activities as kinds of science. This need not be the case.

Our position is that qualitative research conducted as science should complement nonqualitative science. That qualitative research has not built cumulatively on other qualitative research is due in large part to a lack of attention to issues of reliability. In order to make their findings relevant to other findings of whatever sort, qualitative researchers must accept the goal of objectivity, realize the strengths and weaknesses inherent in the ethnographic tradition, and coordinate ethnographic decision making to the four-phase structure of science.

Objectivity (Chapter 1) critically figures in the research arrangement between human observers and humans observed. It is the metaphysical perspective of the authors that reality is something "out there in the real world" and also something "inside our heads." Observations of both phenomena are appropriate to field research.

Qualitative research has gotten bad press for the wrong reasons and good press for the wrong reasons. Complicating the problem, some nonqualitative enthusiasts brand qualitative research as "descriptive," by which they mean nonquantitative. This pejorative use of the term is wrong-headed. Descriptive work can be either qualitative or quantitative (e.g., descriptive statistics). More important is whether or not research of any category—whether qualitative or not—is in some way hypothesis testing. When it is, such work has a potential to modify a scientific paradigm directly. When not, the assembly of "baseline" information makes a different and indirect contribution to the evolution of science.

As do other scientists, qualitative researchers do not report on studied objects (in this instance, cultures) so much as they report on their interaction with the objects. This is why objectivity is difficult, and essential. It is no less possible to be objective in the examination of societies than it is in the investigation of the physical environment. The success of a research effort at achieving objectivity is measured in terms of its validity and reliability.

Perfect validity entails perfect reliability but not the converse; perfect validity is theoretically impossible. Herein lies the paradox of the qualitative tradition. Ethnographers can argue that the good sense of a commitment to validity (Chapter 3), but neglect of reliability (Chapter 5) is scientifically fatal. Overall, the "good news" of a century of sociological and anthropological field research (Chapter 4) is that it has resulted in several fundamental refinements of method. Franz Boas insisted on fieldwork and the collection of primary source data; Bronislaw Malinowski demonstrated the power of ethnographic analysis;

and Robert Park demanded timeliness in reporting out of respect for the research contract. The "bad news" is that little progress was made over the same period in mediating the limitations of qualitative methodologies vis-à-vis reliability.

Qualitative researchers can no longer afford to beg the issue of reliability. While the forte of field research will always lie in its capability to sort out the validity of propositions, its results will (reasonably) go ignored minus attention to reliability. For reliability to be calculated, it is incumbent on the scientific investigator to document his or her procedure. This must be accomplished at such a level of abstraction that the loci of decisions internal to the research project are made apparent. The curious public (or peer reviewer or funding source) deserves to know exactly how the qualitative researcher prepares him- or herself for the endeavor, and how data is collected and analyzed. But the researcher also needs to be able to isolate the conditions under which he or she best "goes to risk"—the time at which he or she is organized to learn something.

The solution proposed here to the scientific problem of talking about reliability and the pragmatic problem of efficiently doing science lies in the adoption of a language for coding the scientific behavior of the researcher. Specifically, qualitative researchers need to know where they are in the research process at different points in time. The novelty of the field and the ambition of researchers to understand the totality of social facts create a "no-win" situation in which the fieldworker must resist the temptation to study all things at once. In short, the qualitative researcher must plan on asking him- or herself "where am I?" and "when am I done?" many times. Not to do so is to risk the research project, as well as the mental health of the researcher.

The four-phase model of the ethnographic process presented in this chapter helps the qualitative researcher make decisions. In the application to work in the field, the model sharply categorizes activities as falling within the purview of either Invention (research design), Discovery (data collection), Interpretation (analysis), or Explanation (documentation). The simple rules of the model (complete a phase before moving to the next phase, complete all phases) do not in themselves guarantee a respectable research project, but they do provide structure and direction pertinent to this objective. Knowing how to code the research activity (or subactivity) at hand, and knowing what other activities bracket it, alert the ethnographer to the phase requirements of science. Thinking about the sequencing of research in terms of moving through phases (or shifting gears or operating in qualitatively different modes) is the necessary first step in reporting about procedure—the topic of most discourse in matters of reliability. The model of science is the only defense a qualitative researcher needs.

It is our argument that qualitative research can be performed as social science and can be evaluated in terms of objectivity. The fundamental gist of this book is that the problem of validity is handled by field research and the problem of reliability is handled by documented ethnographic decision making.

NOTES

1. Most such errors are "hermeneutic," in the sense that they represent misunderstandings of the relationships of parts to wholes.

2. Following the oral tradition of science, we regard "data" as a mass noun like "love" or "jewelry," and assign it a singular verb.

3. See Tukey (1977) and Hartwig and Dearing (1979) for a discussion of a recent trend by statisticians to construct quantitative techniques more appropriate to qualitative research.

4. For well-known introductions to these concepts in the social science and participant observation applications, see, for example, Cronbach and Meehl (1955), Selltiz et al. (1963), Webb et al. (1966), Sjoberg and Nett (1968), and Becker (1970).

5. Bearing in mind that the term "measurement" in many contexts implies the assessment of degree—that is, nonqualitative observation—it will be convenient here to regard qualitative observations as a special case of measurement.

6. The terms reliability and validity are reminiscent of the physical-science notions of precision and accuracy. In physics, "precision" refers to a feature of reporting a measurement—roughly speaking, to the amount of accuracy being claimed. Spurious precision consists of reporting a measurement in such detail that it has neither reliability nor validity. To avoid spurious precision, one restricts the report to the level of specificity at which an accurate statement can be made. Thus both reliability and validity are subsumed under the concept of accuracy.

7. According to Bonjean et al. (1967), Srole's five-question Anomia scale, with 28 independent citations, was the seventh most frequently used measure in sociology during the period 1954-1965.

8. "In making use of the term 'invidious,' it may perhaps be unnecessary to remark, there is no intention to extol or depreciate, or to commend or deplore any of the phenomena which the work is used to characterize. The term is used in a technical sense" (Veblen, 1931: 34).

9. Spradley (1979) used the term "translation competence" to refer to the ethnographically undesirable tendency of informants to provide prepackaged, partyline, and extra-emic answers to questions.

10. Historical treatments of anthropological fieldwork are found in Penniman (1974), Hodgen (1964), and Stocking (1983).

11. A member of the research team, Francois Péron, was perhaps the first paid ethnographic fieldworker. Unfortunately, Péron ignored much of his assigned task, largely because he was a "self-appointed spy" intent on studying British settlements in the spirit of French colonial expansion (Moore, 1969).

12. At Oxford, Tylor was the first Instructor in Anthropology (1883) and first Professor and Lecturer of Anthropology (31 December 1898) in the British Isles. For

reports on early worldwide distributions of the anthropological teaching force, see Dorsey (1894) and MacCurdy (1899, 1902).

13. Nowhere is Tylor cited as actually having conducted fieldwork; however, the circumstances of poor health and a wealthy family resulted in a restorative trip to the New World and a first-hand appreciation of Mexican and tropical cultures. Harris's (1968) opinion is that Morgan's work "would not be considered a bonafide field experience by modern standards, since it did not involve continuous or prolonged contact with the daily routine of a given local community."

14. Freilich (1977) prefers to say anthropology grew "from 'infancy' to 'childhood' " during the period 1860-1900. Kluckhohn (1949: 4) contends that "It would be going too far to call the nineteenth-century anthropology 'the investigation of oddments by the eccentric.' "

15. We have done disservice in this section to Adolf Bastian (1826-1905). Bastian traveled the globe as a ship's surgeon in the mid-1800s; he returned to Berlin to publish his ethnographic findings, became Curator of Ethnography, founded the *Königliches Museum für Völkerkunde*, helped organize the Berlin Society for Anthropology, Ethnography, and Prehistory, and coedited the journal *Zeitschrift für Ethnologie*. Lowie (1937) devotes an entire chapter to Bastian, who must have invented the image of anthropologists as connoisseurs of foreign cultures while terrorizing in their own.

16. Boas's anthropological research among the Baffin Island Eskimo (1883-1884) and Pacific Northwest peoples (Kwakiutl work beginning 1886; the Jesup North Pacific expedition 1897-1902) ranks among the earliest fieldwork on record. Other nineteenth-century fieldworkers include Karl von den Steinen (Brazilian expeditions in 1884 and 1887); the Torres Strait expedition team (A. C. Haddon and associates, 1888 and 1889); and certainly Sir Walter Baldwin Spencer and Frank J. Gillen. By 1899, these last two researchers had spent more than two decades among the Australian Arunta with the consequence that "*both of us are regarded as fully initiated members of the same tribe*" (1904: x).

17. That, as will be shown, the discipline of sociology has contributed its full share to the technology of fieldwork counts for little in the common assumption of both disciplines that cultural anthropologists are somehow the custodians of qualitative methods.

18. Descriptions of the Chicago School as fortified by Park are found in Stein (1960), Madge (1962), and Faris (1967).

19. The rise of the Chicago School was greatly facilitated by the fact that many citizens of Chicago wanted their city understood and were willing to underwrite social research.

20. The terms "participant observation" and "objective observation" are attributed to Lindeman (1924). Interestingly, Anderson (1961) reports that he was unfamiliar with these labels at the time he conducted fieldwork for *The Hobo*. The two men later collaborated (Anderson and Lindeman, 1930).

21. This terminology arises from a Jorge Luis Borges (1964) account of an author who labored to compose the *Quixote* in precisely the same words as Miguel de Cervantes.

22. Perhaps the best resolution of the original debate is that power is something experienced from the bottom, not from the top. It is a common experience to have one's whim frustrated by some person or agency with the power to do so, but a rare experience indeed to be able to impose one's whim on others. Power is indeed exercised, but those who exercise it rarely have the choice about whether or how to do so, for the power only exists by virtue of accommodating those other interests that support it. Naturally, the investigator who interviews and identifies with the powerless will see power in action,

whereas the one who interviews and identifies with the powerful will discover that the untrammeled exercise of power is only a myth.

23. Certain anthropologists (e.g., Brady, 1983) have taken Freeman to be challenging the competence and integrity of one of their culture heroes and favorite people, and have entirely dismissed his work as crude and intended only to shock. This does not appear to have been his intent. Modern ethnography was in its very beginnings at the time of Mead's research, and to criticize her findings out of historical context would be equivalent to criticizing Edison's original light bulb for burning out after a few seconds.

24. Bridgman (1927) is one statement of the position most vulnerable to this kind of error.

25. This extreme is approached, for example, by Mehan and Wood (1976).

26. Friedman (1967) doubts even this in social psychology.

27. These terms, Invention, Discovery, Interpretation, and Explanation, are used as technical terms in the ways defined here. In order to avoid proliferation of jargon, rather more vulgar labels have been used for activities subsumed under these major phases.

GLOSSARY

APPARENT VALIDITY: "Face Validity"—The obviousness of the relationship between an observational procedure and what it is intended to observe. (Chapter 3)

CHECKING THE VALIDITY: An aspect of INTERPRETATION. At issue is whether or not the researcher is calling things by their right names. (Chapter 6)

CHECKING THE RELIABILITY: An aspect of INTERPRETATION. At issue is under what conditions results might be replicated. (Chapter 6)

COPPING DIRECTIONS: An aspect of INVENTION. At issue is the problem of arriving at the field. (Chapter 6)

COPPING A TASTE: At issue is the preliminary and "free-form" exchange between the observer and observed. (Chapter 6)

COPPING A LOOK: An aspect of INVENTION. At issue is the first exposure to a studied culture. (Chapter 6)

DIACHRONIC RELIABILITY: "External Reliability"—The extent to which the same observation made at different times yields the same information. (Chapter 5)

DISCOVERY: "Data Collection"; "Working the field"—The second, "field phase" of qualitative research that distinguishes it from nonqualitative research. (Chapter 6)

EXPLANATION: "Report writing"; "Leaving the field"—The fourth and final phase of scientific research, beginning after data has been collected and analyzed; presentation of a thematic point to a particular audience. (Chapter 6)

FIELD NOTES: Timely and verbatim records kept by a field researcher; may include diary-like material and tentative interpretation. (Chapter 5)

INSTRUMENTAL VALIDITY: "Criterion Validity"—The correspondence between an observation and a different and accepted observation of the same thing. (Chapter 3)

INTERPRETATION: "Analysis"; "Reading the field"—The third phase of scientific research, beginning after an appropriate amount of data has been collected from a particular time and place; organization and summary of data, drawing conclusions from the data. (Chapter 6)

INVENTION: "Research design"; "Finding the field"—The first phase of scientific research, comprising all the activity leading up to the collection of data. (Chapter 6)

OBJECTIVITY: A commitment to integrating new findings into the cumulative body of collective knowledge and confronting ideas with data as well as argument. (Chapter 1)

PHENOMENOLOGY: Emphasis on the process of observation, sometimes to the exclusion of concern for external reality. (Chapter 1)

POSITIVISM: Emphasis on external reality, sometimes to the exclusion of concern for the process of observation. (Chapter 2)

PRAGMATISM: Emphasis on a continuing concern with the observer, the observed, and the activity of observation; manifest in social science under the name "symbolic interactionism." (Chapter 1)

QUALITATIVE RESEARCH: 1. Research involving counting. 2. Research not involving counting. 3. Observation and interaction with the target of study on its own home ground: ethnography, fieldwork, naturalistic research, participant observation. (Chapter 1)

QUIXOTIC RELIABILITY: Multiple observations yielding identical information; in field research often a signal of problems in validity. (Chapter 5)

RELIABILITY: The extent to which the same observational procedure in the same context yields the same information; for the implications of the term "same," see diachronic, quixotic, synchronic reliability. (Chapter 5)

SCORING A CHANCE: An aspect of DISCOVERY. At issue is the securing of the situation to collect data. (Chapter 6)

SCORING AN ENDING: An aspect of DISCOVERY. At issue is knowing when and how to stop collecting data. (Chapter 6)

SCORING THE FACTS: The central aspect of DISCOVERY. At issue is the gathering of data. (Chapter 6)

SPLITTING THE SCENE: An aspect of EXPLANATION. At issue is the consequence of the observer leaving the field. (Chapter 6)

SPLITTING THE TAKE: An aspect of EXPLANATION. At issue is the dividing of research costs and benefits between the observer and the observed. (Chapter 6)

SPLITTING-UP: An aspect of EXPLANATION. At issue is the stopping of data collection activities. (Chapter 6)

SYNCHRONIC RELIABILITY: "Internal Reliability"—The extent to which two simultaneous observations, or two observations of an unchanging target, yield the same information. (Chapter 5)

THEORETICAL VALIDITY: "Construct Validity"—The quality of the relationship between an observation and the element of a model that represents it. (Chapter 3)

VALIDITY: The quality of fit between an observation and the basis on which it is made—see apparent, instrumental, theoretical validity; often the issue is the naming of variables. (Chapter 3)

REFERENCES

ADAMS, R. N. and J. J. PREISS [eds.] (1960) Human Organization Research. Homewood, IL: Dorsey.

AGAR, M. H. (1983) "Ethnographic evidence." Urban Life 12: 32-48.

———(1982) "Toward an ethnographic language." American Anthropologist 84: 779-795.

———(1980) The Professional Stranger. New York: Academic.

ANDERSON, J. R. (1980) Cognitive Psychology and Its Implications. San Francisco: Freeman.

ANDERSON, N. (1961) The Hobo. Chicago: Chicago (orig. pub. 1923).

———and E. C. LINDEMAN (1930) Urban Sociology. New York: Knopf.

BADASH, L. (1965) "Chance favors the prepared mind: Henri Becquerel and the discovery of radioactivity." Archives of the International Historical Society 18: 55-66.

BECKER, H. S. (1970) Sociological Work. Chicago: Aldine.

BERREMAN, G. D. (1966) "Anemic and emetic analysis in social anthropology." American Anthropologist 68: 346-354.

BEVERIDGE, W.I.B. (1950) The Art of Scientific Investigation. New York: W. W. Norton.

BLACK, M. and D. METZGER (1965) "Ethnographic description and the study of law," in L. Nader (ed.) The Ethnography of Law. American Anthropologist 67, 6 (Special Publication, Part 2): 141-165.

BLUMER, H. (1968) Symbolic Interactionism. New York: Prentice-Hall.

BLUMER, M. (1983) "The society for social research," in J. Thomas (ed.) The Chicago School. Urban Life 11, 4 (Special Issue): 421-439.

BONJEAN, C. M., R. J. HILL, and S. D. McLEMORE (1967) Sociological Measurement. San Francisco: Chandler.

BORGES, J. L. (1964) "Pierre Menard, author of the *Quixote*," in Labyrinths. New York: New Directions 36-44.

BOWEN, E. S. [Bohannan, L.] (1954) Return to Laughter. New York: Harper.

BRADY, I. [ed.] (1983) "Speaking in the name of the real: Freeman and Mead on Samoa." American Anthropologist 85, 4 (Special Section): 908-944.

BRIDGMAN, P. W. (1927) The Logic of Modern Physics. New York: Macmillan.

BRIM, J. A. and D. H. SPAIN (1974) Research Design in Anthropology. New York: Holt, Rinehart & Winston.

CARROLL, L. (1960) The Annotated Alice. M. Gardner (ed.) New York: Clarkson N. Potter. (Carroll's book pub. originally in 1865)

CLARK, T. N. (1971) Community Politics. New York: Free Press.

COLEMAN, J. S. (1973) The Mathematics of Collective Action. Chicago: Aldine.

CRONBACH, L. J. and P. E. MEEHL (1955) "Construct validity in psychological tests."
Psychological Bulletin 52, 4: 281-302.

CRUTCHFIELD, R. S. (1955) "Conformity and character." American Psychologist 10:
191-198.

DAHL, R. H. (1961) Who Governs? New Haven, CT: Yale.

DEGERANDO, J. (1969) Considerations on the Various Methods to Follow in the
Observation of Savage People. (F.C.T. Moore, trans.) Berkeley: University of
California. (orig. pub. 1800).

DICKE, R. H., P.J.E. PEEBLES, P. G. ROLL, and D. T. WILKINSON (1965) "Cosmic
black-body radiation." Astrophysical Journal 142: 414-419.

DORSEY, G. A. (1894) "The study of anthropology in American colleges." The
Archaeologist 2: 368-373.

DOUGLAS, J. D. (1976) Investigative Social Research. Beverly Hills, CA: Sage.

DUMONT, J. (1978) The Headman and I. Austin: University of Texas Press.

DURKHEIM, E. (1951) Suicide. (J. Spaulding and G. Simpson, trans.) New York: Free
Press. (orig. pub. 1897).

EAGLY, A. H. (1978) "Sex differences in influenceability." Psychological Bulletin 85:
86-116.

EMERSON, R. M. (1983) "Introduction," part 1 in R. M. Emerson (ed.) Contemporary
Field Research. Boston: Little, Brown.

———(1962) "Power-dependence relations." ASR 27: 31-41.

ETZIONI, A. (1964) Modern Organizations. Englewood Cliffs, NJ: Prentice-Hall.

EVANS-PRITCHARD, E. E. (1951) Social Anthropology. New York: Free Press.

FARIS, R.E.L. (1967) Chicago Sociology 1920-1932. San Francisco: Chandler.

FLEMING, A. (1946) "History and development of penicillin," pp. 1-23 in A. Fleming
(ed.) Penicillin: Its Practical Application. Philadelphia: Blakiston.

FRAKE, C. O. (1964) "Notes and queries on ethnography," in A. K. Romney and R. G.
D'Andrade (eds.) Transcultural Studies in Cognition. American Anthropologist 66, 3
(Special Publication): 132-145, Part 2.

FREEDMAN, J. L., J. M. CARLSMITH, and D. O. SEARS (1970) Social Psychology.
Englewood Cliffs, NJ: Prentice-Hall.

FREEMAN, D. (1983) Margaret Mead and Samoa. Cambridge, MA: Harvard.

FREEMAN, L. C. (1968) Patterns of Local Community Leadership. Indianapolis:
Bobbs-Merrill.

FREILICH, M. [ed.] (1977) Marginal Natives at Work: Anthropologists in the Field. New
York: Wiley.

FRIEDMAN, N. (1967) The Social Nature of Psychological Research. New York: Basic
Books.

GEERTZ, C. (1974) " 'From the native's point of view': on the nature of anthropological
understanding." Bulletin of the American Academy of Arts and Sciences 27-45.

GOLDBERG, P. (1974) "Prejudice toward women." International Journal of Group
Tensions 4: 53-63.

GOLDSCHMIDT, W. (1982) letter to the editor. American Anthropologist 84, 3:
641-643.

GRAFF, G. (1979) Literature Against Itself. Chicago: University of Chicago Press.

HARRIS, M. (1979) Cultural Materialism. New York: Random House.

———(1968) The Rise of Anthropological Theory. New York: Crowell.

HARTWIG, F. and B. E. DEARING (1979) Exploratory Data Analysis. Sage University Paper series on Quantitative Applications in the Social Sciences, 07-16. Beverly Hills: Sage.

HIRSCH, E. D., Jr. (1976) The Aims of Interpretation. Chicago: University of Chicago Press.

HODGEN, M. T. (1964) Early Anthropology in the Sixteenth and Seventeenth Centuries. Philadelphia: Pennsylvania University Press.

HUNTER, F. (1953) Community Power Structure. Chapel Hill: University of North Carolina Press.

JANIS, I. L. and P. B. FIELD (1959) "Sex differences and personality factors related to persuasibility," in C. I. Hovland and I. L. Janis (eds.) Personality and Persuasibility. New Haven, CT: Yale.

JOHNSON, A. W. (1978) Quantification in Cultural Anthropology. Stanford, CA: Stanford University Press.

JUNKER, B. H. (1960) Field Work. Chicago: University of Chicago Press.

KLUCKHOHN, C. (1949) Mirror for Man. New York: McGraw-Hill.

LABOV, W. and P. FANSHEL (1977) Therapeutic Discourse. New York: Academic.

LEACH, E. R. (1967) "An anthropologist's reflection on a social survey," pp. 75-88 in D. C. Jongmans and P. C. Gutkind (eds.) Anthropologists in the Field. Assen: Van Gorcum.

LEVI-STRAUSS, C. (1961) A World on the Wane. (J. Russel, trans.) New York: Criterion Books (orig. pub. 1955).

LINDEMAN, E. C. (1924) Social Discovery. New York: Republic.

LOWIE, R. (1937) The History of Ethnological Theory. New York: Rinehart.

LYND, R. S. and H. M. LYND (1929) Middletown. New York: Harcourt Brace Jovanovich.

MACCOBY, E. E. and C. N. JACKLIN (1974) The Psychology of Sex Differences. Stanford, CA: Stanford University Press.

MACCURDY, G. G. (1902) "The teaching of anthropology in the United States." Science 15, 371: 211-216.

———(1899) "Extent of instruction in anthropology in Europe and the United States." Science 10, 260: 910-917.

MADGE, J. (1962) The Origins of Scientific Sociology. New York: Free Press.

MALINOWSKI, B. (1967) A Diary in the Strict Sense of the Term. (N. Guterman, trans.) New York: Harcourt Brace Jovanovich.

MAQUET, J. J. (1964) "Objectivity in anthropology." Current Anthropology 5: 47-55.

MARCH, J. G. (1966) "The power of power," pp. 39-70 in D. Easton (ed.) Varieties of Political Theory. Englewood Cliffs, NJ: Prentice-Hall.

MEAD, M. (1973) "The art and technology of field work," pp. 246-265 in R. Naroll and R. Cohen (eds.) A Handbook of Method in Cultural Anthropology. New York: Columbia. (orig. pub. 1970).

———(1972) Blackberry Winter. New York: Morrow.

———(1965) Anthropologists and What They Do. New York: Watts.

———(1928) Coming of Age in Samoa. New York: Morrow.

MEHAN, H. and H. WOOD (1976) The Reality of Ethnomethodology. New York: Wiley.

MILLER, C. O., F. SKOOG, M. H. VON SLATZA, and F. M. STRONG (1955) "Kinetin, a cell division factor from Deoxyribonucleic acid." Journal of the American Chemical Society 77: 1392 (communication to the editor).

MOORE, F.C.T. (1969) "Translator's introduction," in J. Degerando, The Observation of Savage Peoples. Berkeley: University of California Press.

MURDOCK, G. P. (1967) Ethnographic Atlas. Pittsburgh: University of Pittsburgh Press.

———(1949) Social Structure. New York: Macmillan.

NUNNALLY, J. (1959) Tests and Measurements. New York: McGraw-Hill.

PALMER, V. (1928) Field Studies in Sociology. Chicago: University of Chicago Press.

PELTO, P. J. and G. H. PELTO (1978) Anthropological Research. New York: Cambridge University Press.

PENNIMAN, T. K. (1974) A Hundred Years of Anthropology. New York: Morrow.

PENZIAS, A. A. and R. W. WILSON (1965) "A measurement of excess antenna temperature at 4080 Mc/s." Astrophysical Journal 142: 419-421.

PIAGET, J. (1954) The Construction of Reality in the Child. (M. Cook, trans.) New York: Basic.

POLSBY, N. W. (1980) Community Power and Political Theory. New Haven, CT: Yale.

POPPER, K. R. (1959) The Logic of Scientific Discovery. New York: Basic.

POWDERMAKER, H. (1966) Stranger and Friend. New York: W. W. Norton.

RABINOW, P. (1977) Reflections on Fieldwork in Morocco. Berkeley: University of California Press.

RAIFFA, H. (1968) Decision Analysis. Reading, MA: Addison-Wesley.

ROSS, L., G. BIERBRAUER, and S. HOFFMAN (1976) "The role of attribution processes in conformity and dissent." American Psychologist 31: 148-157.

Royal Anthropological Institute (1951) Notes and Queries on Anthropology. London: Routledge & Kegan Paul (6th edition).

———(1929) Notes and Queries on Anthropology. London: Author (5th edition).

———(1874) Notes and Queries on Anthropology. London: British Association for the Advancement of Science. (1st edition)

SARKAR, N. K. and S. J. TAMBIAH (1957) The Disintegrating Village. Colombo, Sri Lanka: Ceylon University Socio-Economic Survey of Pata Dumbara.

SEGALL, M. H., D. T. CAMPBELL, and M. H. HERSKOVITS (1966) The Influence of Culture on Visual Perception. Indianapolis: Bobbs-Merrill.

SELLTIZ, C., M. JAHODA, M. DEUTSCH, and S. W. COOK (1963) Research Methods in Social Relations. New York: Holt, Rinehart & Winston.

SISTRUNK, F. and J. W. McDAVID (1971) "Sex variable in conforming behavior." Journal of Personality and Social Psychology 17: 200-207.

SJOBERG, G. and R. NETT (1968) A Methodology for Social Research. New York: Harper & Row.

SMALL, A. W. (1916) "Fifty years of sociology in the United States." American Journal of Sociology 21, 6: 721-864.

SONTAG, S. (1963) "A hero of our time." The New York Review of Books 1, 7: 6-8.

SPENCER, W. B. and F. J. GILLEN (1904) The Northern Tribes of Central Australia. New York: Macmillan.

SPRADLEY, J. P. (1979) The Ethnographic Interview. New York: Holt, Rinehart & Winston.

SROLE, L. (1956) "Social integration and certain corollaries," ASR 21: 709-716.

STEIN, M. R. (1960) The Eclipse cf Community. Princeton, NJ: Princeton University Press.

STOCKING, G. W., Jr. (1983) Observers Observed. Madison: Wisconsin University Press.

TAX, S. (1955) "From Lafitan to Radcliffe-Brown: a short history of the study of social organization," in F. Eggen (ed.) Social Anthropology of North American Tribes. Chicago: Chicago University Press.

TUKEY, J. W. (1977). Exploratory Data Analysis. Reading, MA: Addison-Wesley.

VAN MAANEN, J. (1982) "Fieldwork on the beat," in J. Van Maanen et al. (eds.) Varieties of Qualitative Research. Beverly Hills, CA: Sage. 103-151.

———[ed.] (1979) Qualitative Methodology. Administrative Science Quarterly 24 (Special Issue): 4.

VEBLEN, T. B. (1931) The Theory of The Leisure Class. New York: Modern Library. (orig. pub. 1899)

WARNER, W. L. and P. S. LUNT (1941) The Social Life of a Modern Community. New Haven, CT: Yale University Press.

WEBB, E. J., D. T. CAMPBELL, R. D. SCHWARTZ, and L. SECHREST (1966) Unobtrusive Measures. Chicago: Rand McNally.

WHITING, J.W.M. et al. (1966) Field Guide for a Study of Socialization. Six Cultures Series, Vol. 1. New York: Wiley.

WHYTE, W. F. (1955) Street Corner Society. Chicago: Chicago University Press.

ABOUT THE AUTHORS

JEROME KIRK is Associate Professor of Comparative Sociology and Urban Anthropology at the University of California, Irvine. He received a B.A. in mathematics from Reed College, and a Ph.D. in sociology from The Johns Hopkins University. In pursuit of his interest in collective innovation and social change, he has conducted field research in Polynesia and South America as well as in a wide variety of North American sites. His articles have been published in such journals as *American Anthropologist, American Journal of Sociology, American Political Science Review, American Sociological Review, Anthropological Linguistics, Public Opinion Quarterly*, and *Social Forces*.

MARC L. MILLER is Assistant Professor of Marine Studies and Adjunct Assistant Professor of Anthropology at the University of Washington. He received his Ph.D. from the University of California, Irvine, in 1974. He specializes in the sociology of work and occupations, formal organizations, recreation, leisure, and tourism, and has conducted field research in Mexico, South America, and on the East and West coasts of the United States. He has published in *Coastal Zone Management Journal, Human Organization, New Scholar, Urban Life, Ocean Development and International Law, Social Networks, Work and Occupations*, and *Environment and Behavior*, among other professional journals.